Whippets

WHIPPETS

AN OWNER'S COMPANION

Shirley Rawlings

The Crowood Press

First published in 1991 by
The Crowood Press Ltd
Gipsy Lane, Swindon
Wiltshire SN2 6DQ

British Library Cataloguing in Publication Data

Rawlings, Shirley
  Whippets
  1. Whippets
  I. Title
  636.753

ISBN 1 85223 275 X

Throughout the book, 'he', 'him' and 'his' have been used as
neutral pronouns and refer to both males and females.

Typeset by Photosetting, Yeovil
Printed and bound in Great Britain by
BPCC Hazell Books, Aylesbury

Contents

Dedication

This book is dedicated to my husband who, twenty-five
years ago, agreed rather reluctantly to the
introduction of a whippet into our household.

Acknowledgements

This book would never have been undertaken without encouragement from my husband, and would have been an even more difficult task without the expert editing of Rae Sebley.

I should like to thank my vet Mr S. Blowey, B.Vet.Med., MRCVS, for finding time in his crowded schedule to check the chapter on care, and Mrs Kitchen and Mrs Baker for the information on racing Whippets contained in Chapter 11. Major Loch's contribution to the historical records of Whippet coursing are well known to those in the sport and he has been unstinting in his help in compiling the chapter on coursing Whippets.

A debt of gratitude is also owed to those who have contributed photographs, and the various owners, breeders and photographers who have allowed their work to appear. These are: R. Selbey for the photograph on page 30; D. Webber, pages 34 and 105; Evening Argus Brighton, page 36; J. Hartley, pages 91 and 92; L. Young, page 93; T. Fall, page 98; Whimpanny, pages 99, 101, 115 and 126; Marc Henrie, page 127; J. Meads, pages 118 and 159; E. G. Walsh, pages 123, 124 and 125; and J. Corson, pages 136, 137 and 138. I am particularly grateful to Pedigree Petfoods for permission to reproduce the work of Marc Henrie and Clive Frost.

My thanks also go to Mrs Viv Rainsbury and Mrs Diane Webber for their help in researching the line illustrations for this book.

1

The History of the Breed

The more books on Whippets you read, the more theories and opinions you will find on the origins of the breed. Some authors seek to prove from early paintings and pottery that Whippets have existed as a recognizable breed from the earliest times, while others will state, equally categorically, that the breed only came into being in the late nineteenth century when small Greyhounds were crossed with various terrier breeds to produce a fast little dog for hunting rabbits, and later for racing.

Evidence in Art

There is never any argument about Greyhounds. It is generally agreed that they have existed as a breed for many thousands of years. They are depicted in paintings, on pottery and as statues and are mentioned by name in literature, but when you look carefully at the smaller type of the dogs shown in many of these art forms, it is remarkably like a Whippet both in size, shape and stance. The small bronze Best in Show trophy at the National Whippet Association Championship Show is a copy of the much larger marble Roman statue 'Group of Dogs' which was found at Monte Cagnolo near Lanuvum by Gavin Hamilton and now forms part of the Townley collection in the British Museum. The companion piece to this statue is in the Vatican Museum in Rome. These two dogs are certainly closer in type to the Whippet than to Greyhounds or Italian Greyhounds.

It is also true that there is much artistic proof that dogs which closely resembled the modern Whippet existed in the late seventeenth century. The lovely painting by J. B. Oudry (1686–1755), which is in the Musée Nationale de Fontainebleau, shows a pair of dogs of Whippet size and, more important, of Whippet construction. They have the gentle rise over the loin, the length of back and hind angulation of the Whippet together with the bone and strength one would expect

9

WAMCO BRONZE

The National Whippet Association trophy for Best in Show at the Championship Show is a lovely bronze model, which is based on the marble statue in the Townley collection at the British Museum. The companion piece to this marble is to be found in the Vatican Museum, and they are dated as second century AD.

in a sporting dog. They are neither scaled-down Greyhounds nor over-sized Italian Greyhounds. It might also be assumed that as this pair of dogs was presented to Louis XV, it is unlikely that they were a pair of cross-bred lurchers or mongrels, but prized sporting dogs of recognized parentage.

In the middle of the nineteenth century, the school of artists known as Les Animaliers produced some lovely bronzes of both Whippets and Italian Greyhounds in which the subtle difference between the breeds is shown most clearly. These bronzes have been described in various catalogues as Greyhounds, Whippets and Italian Greyhounds!

10

Development of the Modern Whippet

Man has used dogs to help him while hunting since time immemorial and different types of hound have evolved to deal with the various quarries. Larger, heavier hounds would have been needed to deal with wolves or wild boar, but in areas where small deer, rabbits or hare

'Lady with a Whippet' *by F. R. de Leub, a nineteenth-century Belgian artist. Gift of Mrs Paul R. Willemsen to The Dog Museum of St Louis.*

were hunted, the speedier, more agile Greyhound type would have been more suitable. The more enclosed the area, the smaller would have been the preferred size of Greyhound.

Towards the end of the eighteenth century, the medium-sized running dog appears to have acquired a name of his own – the 'whippet' or 'snap dog' – and was a popular breed amongst the working men in the north of the country. These dogs were used for rabbit coursing and later for racing to the rag. This form of so-called 'coursing' bore no resemblance to the coursing of hares under National Coursing Club rules, but it is probably responsible for many of the misconceptions held about the sport today. It is not possible to course rabbits in the way that hares are coursed as they rarely emerge more than thirty yards (9 metres) from their burrows, so therefore, the rabbits were netted and then released into enclosures for the dogs to chase. The dogs would be expected to run twenty-five or thirty times a day, so Bull Terrier or Manchester Terrier crosses were introduced to achieve the greater strength and stamina.

The scandals that resulted from rabbit coursing caused this sport to fall into disrepute, and the reputation of the little dogs involved also suffered. The men of the north turned to rag racing their Whippets, and the infusion of terrier blood ceased as speed again became the criterion. Then, as now, there was a handicapping system in Whippet racing based on weight, which advantaged the smaller, lighter-boned dog. The favoured weight for a racing Whippet was around 16 to 17 pounds (7 to 8 kilograms), whereas the rabbit coursing Whippet had weighed in at about 25 pounds (11 kilograms).

Whippets had become known as 'the poor man's Greyhound' and were highly prized possessions, living curled up by the fire and, it is said, often fed rather better than members of the family. They were expected to earn their keep at race meetings where much betting took place, so a dog that lacked speed would not be considered of any value. Only the best bitches would be bred from, and only the fastest dogs used at stud so, once more, the Greyhound type of animal predominated and the Whippet quickly reverted to type.

It is interesting to wonder whether some of the show faults that crop up from time to time in the breed, such as upright ear carriage and broad chests with an upright set to the shoulders, could be traced back to the years when such cross breeding took place. There is certainly little other evidence of the introduction of terrier blood.

In their book, *The English Whippet*, E. G. Walsh and Mary Lowe put forward the fascinating theory that 'with selective breeding from the

Water-colour featured in the Illustrated London News *on
Saturday, 9 March 1912 by their 'Special Artist', Cyrus Cuneo. It
was entitled* 'Miners Amusing Themselves While the Country
Fears – Strikers Whippet Racing'.

same genetic pool, one could, in a few generations, produce an Italian greyhound and a greyhound from original whippet stock'. I would
certainly agree with them that the over-size Whippet looks and gal-
lops like a Greyhound, and the tiny 16-pound (7-kilogram) racing
Whippet often has the rounded skull and fine bone of the Italian Greyhound. All three breeds must have the same genetic make-up and have
evolved in their various ways to fulfil the needs of man.

The Early Breeders

By 1890, the Whippet had become sufficiently popular as a show dog to be officially recognized by the Kennel Club, and in 1896 the first Challenge Certificates were granted. Whippets began to be bred not only for their working ability but for their looks. We should be very grateful to those early breeders, such as Mr H. Bottomley (of the Shirley prefix), Mr A. Lamotte (Manorley), Mr W. Beara (Willes) and Mr W. Lewis-Renwick (Watford) that they never lost sight of the need to maintain the functional ability of the Whippet. It is owing to their dedication and to those that came after them that today's Whippet is still capable of fulfilling the task for which he was originally bred, and is therefore free from the hereditary faults which beset so many other pedigree dogs.

There are excellent chapters on historic Whippet kennels in books by B. S. Fitter, Fitch Daglish, C. H. Douglas-Todd and W. Lewis-Renwick, which give detailed information on the early days of recorded Whippet breeding. The more recently published book by Bo Bengtson entitled simply *The Whippet* also has a carefully researched and informative chapter on the early show Whippets. The photographs in these books have much to interest the historian: though some of the early champions may seem a little unbalanced to a modern eye, many of them look capable of being as successful today as they were then.

Post World War II

After the difficult years of the war, there was a great resurgence in dog breeding, and Whippets became more and more popular. The standard of champion Whippets from these years was extremely high and there was a great depth of quality in the breed. Many of the most famous of the kennels in these years were based on the breeding of Stanley Wilkins (Tiptree). Stanley Wilkins was a firm believer in linebreeding and although he had little success in the show ring during his lifetime, and never owned a champion, his dogs provided a firm basis for later breeders. The Sapperly, Samema, Laguna, Allways and Wingedfoot champions were nearly all descended from Tiptree stock.

Kennel Club registrations for Whippets increased from just over a hundred in 1942 to approximately seven hundred by 1947. From then on, the number of puppies registered each year grew until in 1965 it reached the two thousand mark. This growth was not welcomed by knowledgeable breeders who were only too well aware of the dangers inherent in a breed's becoming too popular. Too many litters bred entirely for profit from inferior bitches result in a general deterioration of quality. However, the dreaded increase did not materialize and the number of litters has remained fairly constant ever since, with about fifteen hundred Whippets registered annually. Even this number is probably too great if judged by the amount of work undertaken by the JR Whippet Rescue (*see* Appendix 1).

The Breed Clubs

The growth in interest in Whippets is reflected in the number of breed clubs formed by enthusiasts of the breed. The earliest of these was The Whippet Club, founded in 1898. The influence of this club was enormous during those early years, and it has been very well served by a long line of dedicated Honorary Secretaries and hard-working committee members. Some of the most famous names in Whippets have served at one time or another on the committee of this club. It is still considered the 'senior partner' of the breed clubs, and, as well as holding one of the most prestigious of the Breed Championship Shows every year, The Whippet Club controls all pedigree Whippet racing in the United Kingdom through The Whippet Club Racing Association.

The National Whippet Association was formed in 1936 with a membership of six and capital of £2! However, the club grew rapidly and is credited with doing a great deal to keep the interest in Whippets alive during the war. It was the NWA who held one of the first shows after the war, in October 1945, and the club was granted Championship Status in 1946. The catalogues for NWA Championship Shows since 1973 are of particular interest to those concerned with the history of the breed, for they contain three-generation pedigrees of all dogs entered.

The third breed club to appear was The Midland Whippet Club (1949), followed in 1955 by The Northern Counties Whippet Club and in 1959 by The Whippet Club of Scotland. There are now ten breed clubs serving all areas of the United Kingdom, and these have formed a Breed Council in order that they may speak with one voice to the Kennel Club, and better serve the majority of Whippet owners.

The breed is fortunate in that so many of its successful and dedicated breeders and exhibitors are willing to give their time and expertise to help run the breed clubs. Novice owners who are members of a breed club need never lack help and advice of the highest order.

The UK Breed Standard

(Reproduced by kind permission of
the Kennel Club of Great Britain)

General Appearance

Balanced combination of muscular power and strength with elegance and grace of outline. Built for speed and work. All forms of exaggeration should be avoided.

Characteristics

An ideal companion. Highly adaptable in domestic and sporting surroundings.

Temperament

Gentle, affectionate, even disposition.

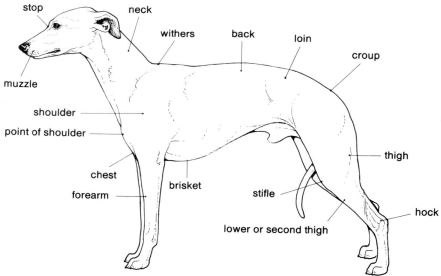

Points of a Whippet. It helps to know the correct name for the various parts of the body when interpreting the Standard for the breed.

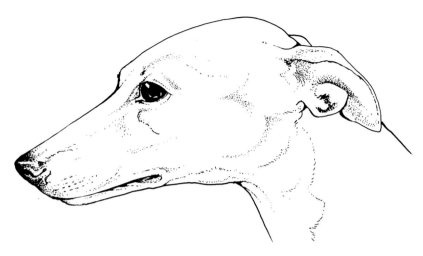

The characteristic head of the Whippet.

Head and Skull

Long and lean, flat on top tapering to muzzle with slight stop, rather wide between the eyes, jaws powerful and clean cut, nose black, in blues a bluish colour permitted, in livers a nose of the same colour, in whites or parti-colour a butterfly nose permissible.

Eyes

Oval, bright, expression very alert.

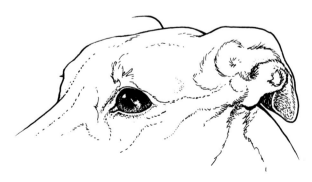

Whippets are 'sighthounds' and have exceptionally good eyesight for a dog.

17

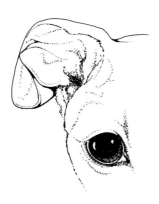
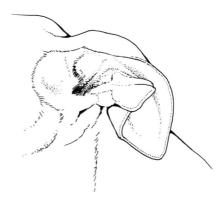

The ears are generally carried flat against the head except when alert, when they should be half-pricked.

Ears

Rose shaped, small, fine in texture.

Mouth

Jaws strong with a perfect, regular and complete scissor bite, i.e. the upper teeth closely overlapping the lower teeth and set square to the jaws.

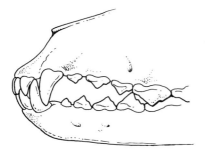
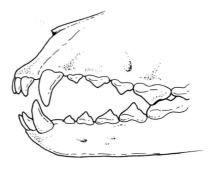

A strong underjaw and correct bite are essential in any hunting dog.

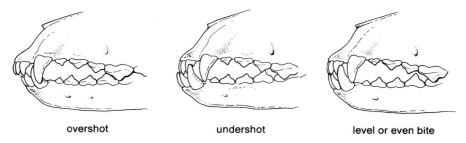

| overshot | undershot | level or even bite |

Incorrect bites. All of these would prevent a Whippet from obtaining a firm grip on his quarry.

Neck

Long, muscular, elegantly arched.

Forequarters

Shoulders oblique and muscular, blades carried up to the top of spine, where they are clearly defined. Forelegs straight and upright, front not too wide, pasterns strong with slight spring, elbows set well under body.

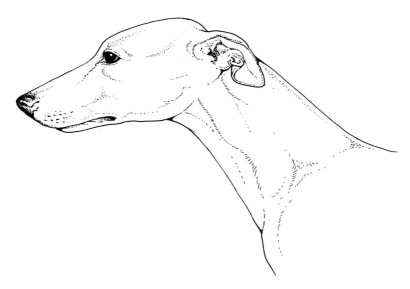

Originally necessary so that he could catch and hold his quarry, the length of neck gives the Whippet great elegance.

19

The oblique set of shoulder-
blade facilitates a long
forward stride, and a slight
spring of pastern acts as a
shock absorber at the gallop,
preventing too great a strain
on feet and legs. A galloping
animal needs heart room
without loss of forward
propulsion.

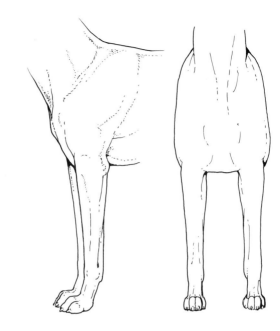

Good length but without
exaggeration is called for –
the outline should be of a
balanced animal.

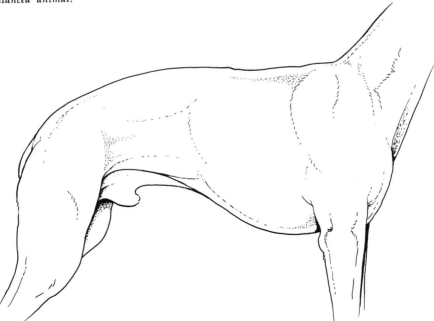

Body

Chest very deep with plenty of heart room, brisket deep, well defined, broad back, firm, somewhat long, showing definite arch over loin, but not humped. Loin giving impression of strength and power, ribs well sprung, muscled on back.

Hindquarters

Strong, broad across thighs, stifles well bent, hocks well let down, well developed second thigh, dog able to stand over a lot of ground and show great driving power.

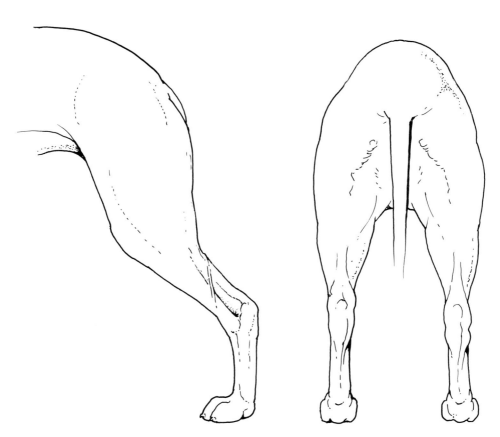

Strong hindquarters provide the power for a running dog, and a good bend of stifle enables a Whippet to turn quickly.

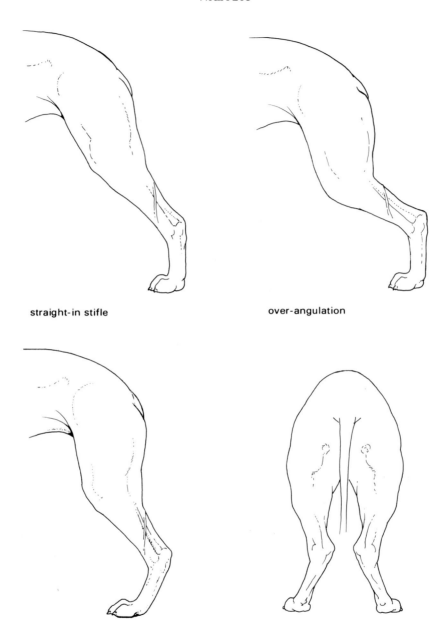

straight-in stifle

over-angulation

sickle hocks

cow hocks

Any of the faults illustrated here are indicative of weakness in the hindquarters, preventing the dog from galloping at great speed and making the possibility of injury more likely.

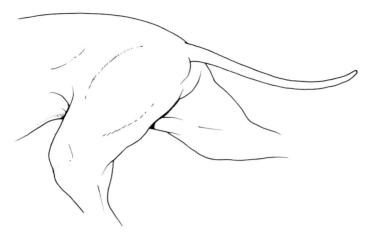

The long tail is used as a rudder, and all the old punters used to say that when in doubt you should back the dog with the longest tail. A short tail detracts from the elegant outline of a Whippet.

Tail

No feathering, long, tapering, when in action carried in a delicate curve upward but not over back.

Feet

Very neat, well split up between toes, knuckles well arched, pads thick and strong.

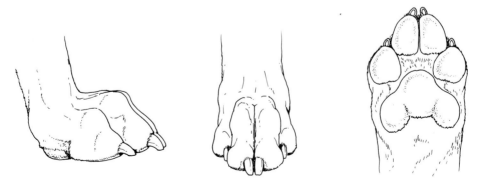

An essential part of a running dog, often overlooked by judges.

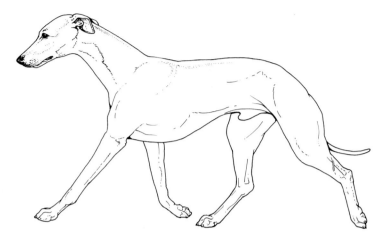

Often called 'daisy-cutting', this long free stride is a characteristic of the breed. The slightly arched topline should be retained whilst on the move.

Gait/Movement

Free, hind legs coming well under body for propulsion. Forelegs thrown forward low over the ground, true coming and going. General movement not to look stilted, high stepping, short or mincing.

Coat

Fine, short, close in texture.

Colour

Any colour or mixture of colours.

Size

Height: Dogs 47–51 cm (18½–20 in). Bitches 44–47 cm (17½–18½in).

Faults

Any departure from the foregoing points should be considered a fault and the seriousness with which the fault should be regarded should be in exact proportion to its degree.

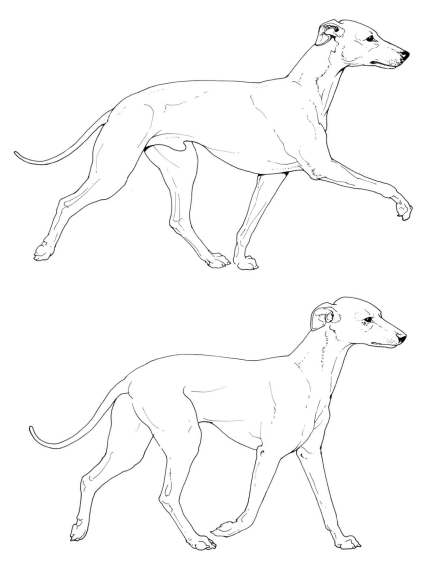

The Standard for the breed specifically mentions both these faults as being uncharacteristic of a Whippet.

Note

Male animals should have two apparently normal testicles fully scended into the scrotum.

25

The American Breed Standard

(Reproduced by kind permission of the American Kennel Club)

General Appearance

A moderate size sight hound giving the appearance of elegance and fitness, denoting great speed, power, and balance without coarseness. A true sporting hound that covers a maximum of distance with a mininum of lost motion.

Head

Long and lean, fairly wide between the ears, scarcely perceptible stop, good length of muzzle which should be powerful without being coarse. Nose entirely black.

Ears

Small, fine in texture, thrown back and folded. Semipricked when at attention. Gay ears are incorrect and should be severely penalized.

Eyes

Large, dark, with keen intelligent alert expression. Lack of pigmentation around eyelids is undesirable. Yellow or dilute-colored eyes should be strictly penalized. Blue or china-colored eyes shall disqualify. Both eyes must be of the same color.

Muzzle

Muzzle should be long and powerful denoting great strength of 'bite' without coarseness. Teeth should be white and strong. Teeth of upper jaw should fit closely over teeth of lower jaw creating a strong scissors bite. Extremely short muzzle or lack of underjaw should be strictly penalized. An even bite is extremely undesirable. Undershot shall disqualify. Overshot one-quarter inch or more shall disqualify.

Neck

Long, clean and muscular, well arched with no suggestion of throatiness, widening gracefully into the top of the shoulder. A short thick neck, or concave curvature of the top neckline sometimes called ewe (opposite of arched), should be penalized.

Shoulders

Long, well laid back, with flat muscles, allowing for moderate space between shoulder blades at the peak of withers. The length of the shoulder blade equals the length of the upper arm. A straight shoulder blade, short upper arm, a heavily muscled or loaded shoulder, or a very narrow shoulder, all restricting low free movement, should be strictly penalized.

Brisket

Very deep and strong, reaching as nearly as possible to the point of the elbow. Ribs well sprung but with no suggestion of barrel shape. Should fill in the space between the forelegs so that there is no appearance of a hollow between them.

Back and Loin

The back broad, firm and well muscled, having length and a strong natural arch over the loin, creating a definite tuck-up of the underline. A short loin creating a cramped stance should be penalized.

Topline and Croup

The topline runs smoothly from the withers with a graceful and not too accentuated arch beginning over the loin and carrying through over the croup, with the arch being continuous without flatness. A wheelback, flat back, dip behind shoulder blades, or a back that falls away sharply creating a cut-away appearance should be penalized. A steep or flat croup should be penalized.

Forelegs

Straight, giving appearance of strength and substance of bone. The points of the elbows should point neither in nor out, but straight back. When the dog moves, the joints allow free movement from the point of the shoulder to give a long low reach. Pasterns strong, slightly bent and flexible. Bowed legs, tied-in elbows, legs lacking substance, legs set far under the body so as to create a forechest, weak or straight pasterns should be strictly penalized.

Feet

Feet must be well formed with hard, thick pads and strong nails. Nails naturally short or of moderate length. Toes should be long, close and well arched. Feet more hare than cat, but both are acceptable. Flat, open, or soft feet without thick hard pads, should be strictly penalized.

Hindquarters

Long and powerful, stifles well bent, hocks well let down and close to the ground. Thighs broad and muscular. The muscles are long and flat and carry well down toward the hock. Sickle or cowhocks should be strictly penalized.

Tail

The tail long and tapering, reaching to the hipbone when drawn through behind the hind legs. When the dog is in motion, the tail is carried low with a gentle upward curve; tail should not be carried higher than top of back. A curled tail should be penalized.

Coat and Color

Short, close, smooth and firm in texture. Any other coat shall be a disqualification. Color immaterial.

Gait

Low, free moving and smooth, with reach in the forequarters and strong drive in the hindquarters. The dog has great freedom of action when viewed from the side; the forelegs reach forward close to the ground; the hind legs have strong propelling power. Lack of front reach or rear drive, a short, mincing gait with high knee action should be strictly penalized. When moving and viewed from front or rear, legs should turn neither in nor out, nor should feet cross or interfere with each other. Crossing in front or moving too close should be strictly penalized.

N.B. Old scars and injuries, the result of work or accident should not be allowed to prejudice the dog's chance in the show ring, unless they interfere with its movement or ability to perform.

Size

Ideal height for dogs, 19 to 22 inches; for bitches, 18 to 21 inches, measured across the shoulders at the highest point. One-half inch above or below the above stated measurements will disqualify.

Disqualifications

Blue or china-colored eyes.
Undershot.
Overshot one-quarter inch or more.
Coat – Other than short, close, smooth and firm in texture.
A dog one-half inch above or below the measurements specified under 'Size'.

2

Why a Whippet?

The decision to join the ranks of those whose lives are made more complicated and restricted by pets is not to be undertaken lightly. There is no doubt that owning a dog does place restrictions on the freedom to come and go. Dogs have to be fed, exercised, groomed and, above all, loved, every day of the year, Christmas and Bank Holidays included. It matters not whether you feel like getting out of your chair, because when supper or walk time comes around, your furry friend will be there looking at you expectantly – and don't let anyone tell you that they cannot talk! The National Canine Defence League's slogan, often seen on car stickers, says 'A Dog Is For Life – Not Just For Christmas', and this maxim ought to be borne in mind by those about

Whippets enjoy a little conversation. Pan chatting to his owner.

to buy a dear little cuddly puppy, whatever the time of year. Do think long and carefully about the characteristics you require from a companion who will be sharing your home and hearth for many years to come.

It stands to reason that I am biased in favour of pure-bred dogs and, in particular, in favour of Whippets. I consider that it is more sensible to buy a pure-bred puppy from a reliable breeder because you will have some idea of the size and characteristics of the adult dog. Much has been written, often by people who should know better, on the virtues of owning mongrels. According to such pundits, mongrels are more likely to be healthy and free from hereditary diseases. Exactly what foundation they have for these beliefs is often somewhat vague, and as the lineage of mongrels is obviously unknown, how can anyone tell what genes they may, or may not, have inherited?

However, it is also undoubtedly true that certain breeds carry the tendency to certain inherited diseases, such as hip dysplasia and progressive retinal atrophy, which is why I stress that it is always better to obtain your puppy from a reliable breeder rather than from an advertisement placed in the local paper by someone about whom you know nothing. The Kennel Club will give you the name and address of the secretaries of the various breed clubs and they can usually put you in touch with well-known and reputable breeders in your area. It is both distressing and expensive to discover that a recently acquired and dearly loved pet is suffering from a condition that cannot be cured and will become progressively worse as he gets older.

Whippets are medium-sized dogs, with short coats and a reasonably light build. As such, they rarely frighten small children by overwhelming them with sheer size. From time to time, I take my Whippets to the school where I teach, and even the most timid child will pluck up the courage to pat their sleek heads. In fact, one five year old, when asked what he wanted for his birthday, stated firmly that he wanted a Whippet. His mother protested that he had never liked dogs, whereupon he said, in a voice of scorn, that he did not want a dog – he wanted a Whippet!

Temperament

This does not mean that you should allow small children to maul young puppies or adult dogs for that matter, but Whippets have a very even temperament and growl or snap only under extreme provocation. It

Some, like Max, are very good at washing up.

is in fact very important in the socialization of any puppy, Whippet or not, that he or she should be introduced to children and handled by children, from nine weeks onwards. Both puppy and child should be supervised so that neither becomes over-excited, but the puppy needs to get used to the higher pitch of children's voices and their sudden and often more uncontrolled gestures, and the child needs to be taught the right way to handle a young puppy and to appreciate when the puppy is tired and wants to go back to his basket. Just as in humans, how a dog grows up depends to a great extent on his upbringing.

Neither are the vast majority of Whippets aggressive towards other dogs. Like most animals blessed with great speed, they prefer to use their speed to avoid a fight and in fact they avoid other dogs.

Size

In general, Whippet bitches vary in height between 17 and 19½ inches (43 and 50 centimetres) at the shoulder, and the dogs between 18½ and 21 inches (47 and 53 centimetres). Their weights go from about

17 pounds to 32 pounds (7.5 to 14.5 kilograms). Obviously a 17-inch bitch is on the small side and a dog of 22 is definitely over size!

For show purposes, a bitch should be between 18 and 19 inches (45 and 48 centimetres) and a dog between 18½ and 20 inches (47 and 51 centimetres), though there are many top-winning Whippets an inch or more than the ideal. There is a strictly enforced top limit of 21 inches (53 centimetres) and a top weight of 30 pounds (13.5 kilograms) for Whippets racing under Whippet Club Racing Association rules. Even more strictly enforced is the National Whippet Coursing Club's height limit of 20 inches (51 centimetres), though there is no weight restriction on coursing dogs as they are not subject to any handicapping system, and no dog fit enough to course would be carrying any vast amount of excess weight.

For most owners, the size of their Whippet is of no great importance and it certainly does not change the nature of the beast, but there is no doubt that from the aesthetic point of view – and Whippets are very pleasing on the eye – too much size detracts from the elegance of the breed type. Personally, and it is only a personal preference, I do not care much for the very small, light-boned Whippet either though I know many who say they are the best of all – 'proper breed dogs'.

Dog or Bitch?

In many breeds, it is generally considered that a bitch makes a better house pet than a dog, but this is not necessarily the case with Whippets. Whippet bitches can be somewhat feline in their nature, more aloof than a dog and less inclined to join in games of chasing sticks or balls. The dogs are more outgoing and friendly, more obedient and they rarely go off looking for extra-curricular activities. A well-known Whippet breeder and exhibitor once wrote in an article: 'no Whippet bitch ever came when she was called unless there was something in it for her' – a comment that caused many an understanding chuckle from other Whippet owners. Certainly there is no more loyal or loving companion than a Whippet dog.

Exercise

As a breed, the Whippet is remarkably free from hereditary diseases. In fact, Whippets are much tougher than they look, and will happily go for a walk in weather that would deter most owners. The Kennel Club Standard describes the Whippet as 'an ideal companion', and so he is. They are very loving and affectionate and remarkably little trouble in the house. Being high on the leg, they bring in relatively little dirt even after an energetic walk, and they have short coats which require only the minimum of grooming to keep in trim. Whippets have been described as the lazy man's dog, which is true in that they are an easy breed to look after and to feed, but they do need daily exercise, though hardly the amounts some prospective owners fear.

If your Whippet is a family pet and not expected to spend an afternoon racing at top speed round a race-track chasing a lure, or a full day walking over heavy plough searching for hares, the amount of exercise he needs can be adjusted to suit your life-style. Like most dogs, half an hour's brisk walk on the roads on a lead will keep him healthy and reasonably fit but being a Whippet, with an in-built need to run, he will appreciate fifteen minutes' free running when he can really stretch out. Most Whippets, when let off the lead in a field or park, will chase round and round and let off steam, coming back very pleased with themselves and quite ready to go home and settle down in front of the fire. It has to be remembered though that Whippets will chase, and you have to be careful where and when you release your dog. A piece of fur tied on the end of a string and swung round

Whippets enjoy a game with a friend, though the cat finds it less amusing.

Whippets have an in-built need to run. Chyton Bonne Chance gets rid of some excess energy.

from a long pole provides lots of chasing and running if fields are full of sheep, or parks full of large dogs of uncertain temperament.

The Kennel Club Standard goes on to say that Whippets are highly adaptable in domestic and sporting surroundings. There are all too few breeds where the same dog will be a loving, docile family pet, an elegant, immaculate show dog and a brave and courageous sporting hound. Your Whippet will thoroughly enjoy an afternoon at the race-track, yapping and barking, pulling and straining at the lead, all to chase a piece of rag pulled on the end of a string and catch it before the other dogs. He knows perfectly well that it is only a piece of rag, but considers the whole thing enormous fun.

Showing

The same dog will spend a day quietly on his show bench, being taken off to be groomed and paraded and 'gone over' by a judge and expected to stand still, posed like a statue, for considerable periods of time while the judge makes his decision.

I cannot believe that most Whippets really enjoy showing, though some, usually kennel dogs whose only day out it may be, give a very

If necessary, a Whippet can make his own amusement. Ballagan Whipcord, top sire of winning puppies in 1986, forgets his heavy responsibilities.

good impression of doing so. Most Whippets are so obliging that they can forgive their owners most things, even being asked to show, and the one thing they do enjoy about showing is the amount of time and attention they receive. Anyone lucky enough to own a show quality Whippet who does like shows has a jewel indeed, for that extra quality of showmanship will win him many classes.

Field Sports

If you are interested in field sports you can take your Whippet coursing, and he will walk all day, often in dreadful weather as the coursing season is late September to early March. The terrain is sometimes very heavy and hares can be scarce. To add insult to injury in the dog's eyes, he is only released when the hare has a lead of at least 35 yards (32 metres) and often more. Oddly enough, Whippets, with certain exceptions, do not bark much while out coursing except when the hare first gets up, and most do not pull particularly hard. Coursing, in the opinion of the Whippet, is a serious business and the frivolities of the race-track must be put aside.

All these things, or none, will your Whippet be – it depends on you and your choice of leisure activities. The only things essential for every Whippet are warmth, a moderate amount of food and exercise, and human companionship and affection. If he lacks the last of these he will be a very sad little Whippet and you have chosen the wrong breed.

A word of warning, however, for those who seek dual or multi-purpose Whippets. They will provide you with much sport and fun, often having particularly lovely temperaments, but it is only rarely that dual champions are born. If you want your dog to excel particu-larly in one area you must choose him with that in mind.

The very best way to find this 'ideal' Whippet if you have already seen the type, colour and size you like, is to ask the owner the name of the breeder and contact him direct. Most owners are very happy to tell you all about their dog, whether it is a Whippet or a mongrel.

Finding a Breeder

If you do not already know someone with a Whippet, the Kennel Club will give you the name of the secretary of one of the breed clubs, of which there are ten at the moment (*see* Appendix 1). Most of the clubs are regionally based, but The Whippet Club and The National Whippet Association consider themselves to have a more national role. The Whippet Club is also the parent club of the Whippet Club Racing Association, which controls all pedigree Whippet racing in the country.

The secretary of any of the breed clubs should be able to give you the name and telephone number of breeders in your area who might have a suitable puppy and, provided that you telephone at a reason-able hour, they will be very happy to talk to you. It is best not to be in too much of a hurry in making your choice; as they tell you in the army, 'time spent in reconnaissance is never wasted'. If you can get to a Breed Show you will see a great variety of types and colours of Whippets and then, having seen the Whippet that appeals to you, you can approach the owner, ask about the dog and enquire whether he might be contemplating breeding a litter from similar blood-lines in the near future.

The same approach applies if you are seeking a Whippet for racing: go to a race meeting, watch what goes on and talk to the people at the track about reliable breeders. The secretaries of racing clubs are usually very busy during the racing, but if you go early, or stay on when the action is over and the track and equipment cleared away, you will find them ready and willing to give you advice. (*See also* Appendix 2.)

It is in your own best interest, as well as the breeder's, to be honest with him about your hopes for your puppy. There is nothing more frustrating for a breeder than to hear exhibitors complain that the dog they assured the breeder was only wanted as a pet cannot win in the ring; or equally, that the puppy they bought from strictly show stock, cannot win a race. Nor is there anything more satisfying than when a puppy bearing your prefix does well in the ring, on the track or in the sporting field. There are breeders who concentrate entirely on one area of Whippet activity and there are those of us who believe that Whippets should be capable of taking part successfully in two or more activities. It is up to you to choose the kennel that can provide you with the Whippet to suit you.

Choosing a Puppy

Having decided on the type of Whippet you like and found a breeder who has a litter of puppies, you have the most difficult decision to make. Contrary to expectations, Whippet puppies do not look like mice: they are, or should be, plump, jolly little souls who come racing up to talk to you, ready to have a game, chew shoe-laces or indulge in any other of the usual puppy activities. Sometimes the decision is made for you in that a puppy decides that he likes you, asks to be picked up and you just know that that is the dog you have to have. Often it is much more difficult to make a choice. If you seek a specialist dog, listen carefully to the advice of the breeder. If you are after a family pet, it is the temperament of the puppy which is the most important (if you have children, a dog puppy with an outgoing character might be the wisest choice). If you want a quiet companion, one of the less boisterous pups might suit you better. Pick the puppy you like best, collect his diet sheet, pedigree, Kennel Club Registration Certificate and any other relevant papers and take him home.

Probably the most difficult to choose is the potential show Whippet, and the advice of the breeder should be taken seriously, though

*Look for a puppy who strides out well. This little fellow shows
promise of moving out like his great grandfather, Ch. Welstar
Royal Mint see photograph on page 114).*

the ultimate responsibility for the decision must be yours. The older
the puppy, the easier it is to see what the adult dog will look like. No
one can guarantee any puppy for the ring – there is so much that can
go wrong at various stages. So if you want a certain show prospect,
it might be sensible to consider buying a youngster already in the ring.
A Whippet will move home without too much trauma up to a year
old, especially if he has been out in a kennel, or part of a large pack
of dogs, and the move means that he becomes a house dog or one of
only two or three animals.

   If you are picking a show puppy at a tender age, do have a good
look at the sire and the dam as well as at the pedigree and at the puppy
himself. Puppies, like children, are inclined to grow up to look like
their parents or at least to have similar characteristics. So, if both parents are rather short in the loin, or their hind movement is incorrect,
the chances are that their offspring will inherit this tendency. When
deciding on a show prospect, a good length of back and neck, strong
bone and a nice four-square way of standing are about all you can go
on. Spend some time watching the litter so that you can see which
puppies stride out well on the move. Do not pick a pup that runs off

39

to hide in the kennel when you appear – such a one is unlikely to have a good show temperament. Otherwise you just have to pick a puppy that you like the look of and whose character appeals, and hope that you have got it right. Every breeder can tell you tales of puppies they discarded only to see them turn into absolute stunners, and of 'certain champions' they kept who never made the grade.

In some ways, picking a potential running Whippet is less problematical in that such characteristics as determination and courage are easier to assess in a youngster than are future show faults. Good basic conformation is just as essential in the working dog as it is in the show dog if he is not to injure himself while running under stress, so do not choose a puppy with an obvious fault. Once again, spend time watching the whole litter. Often it is the puppy who plays 'hare' rather than 'hound' that is the fastest. Play with them. The one you want will come back again and again, even when getting tired, to have a look for the ball or piece of fur.

Bear in mind while making your choice that there is a height limit for sporting dogs, and thus the size of the sire and dam has extra significance. It is probably unwise to decide upon the largest dog pup in the litter when looking for a coursing Whippet if the sire is 21 inches (53 centimetres) high. Another point to remember with a sporting Whippet is that it is considered unwise on health grounds to run a bitch during the twelve weeks after she comes into season. If the number of dogs you can keep is restricted, you have to consider whether you want to have a bitch if she is likely to spend some considerable time of every year off the track or field.

Once you have chosen your puppy and taken him home, forget about all the things he is going to be and do when he is an adult. Look after him properly, rear him sensibly and by the time he has been a member of the family for a month you will not be able to remember how peaceful life was before he arrived. The specialist training for the show ring, race-track or coursing field must take second place to bringing him up to be a well-mannered and sensible dog, and constant assessment of potential show faults, about which you can do nothing, will only detract from your enjoyment of his puppyhood. All puppies go through stages when you wonder if you bought a pure-bred Whippet, let alone one with show potential or the ability to catch a lure. Let him grow up in his own time and he will probably do all and more than you expected.

3

Puppy Care and Training

There are varying opinions as to the best age for a puppy to go to his new home and there is no easy answer. Certainly, the stress caused by removing a tiny puppy from his environment and the comfort of his brothers and sisters is great, and care is needed if the change is to cause as little disturbance to his development as possible. Few Whippet breeders like their youngsters to leave the nest before eight weeks, and many would prefer to keep them to nine or ten weeks before allowing them to go to new homes. There is nothing to be gained by too early a move. That is not to say that you cannot pick out your puppy at five or six weeks if the breeder is happy with this arrangement, but it would be better to pay a deposit on your chosen pup and collect him when he is a few weeks older and more able to cope with such an upheaval in his young life.

When you do collect the puppy, you should be given his pedigree and diet sheet. If the breeder has been very efficient, you may also be given his Kennel Club Registration Certificate, on the back of which is the form for transferring him into your name on the Kennel Club Register. You and the breeder must sign this and you then send it to the Kennel Club with the appropriate fee. You will receive a new certificate with your name as the owner. The initial registration can take some time and you may have to wait a few weeks for this to come through from the Kennel Club.

Most breeders will give you two or three days' supply of food for the puppy in order that you do not have to make any changes to his normal diet. Nowadays, many puppies come with six weeks' insurance cover, for which you will be given a cover note. Do check how often the puppy has been wormed, which worming compound was used and when the last dose was given. All puppies are born with worms and it is most important that these parasites are kept under control or the puppy will not thrive, and there is the risk of danger to the health of humans. This risk, always slight, can be eliminated if the dog is kept free of worms by regular worming. Worming should

41

always be supervised by your vet as you can damage the puppy's intestines by over-use of too strong a substance.

Taking the Puppy Home

If you are taking your puppy home by car, a plastic bag, a roll of kitchen paper and a towel are sensible precautions, as not all breeders have the time to car train their puppies; and if you did not give sufficient warning of your time of arrival, the pup may also have just had a large meal. Some Whippets love travelling by car and leap in whenever a door is opened, but others need to be introduced to it carefully and may take a little time to adjust to the world whizzing by. Sometimes it helps if you can prevent them from looking out of the window, and there are various herbal remedies for travel sickness.

Once you have him home, the best way to cure a car-sick youngster is to take him for very short journeys every day, preferably with a treat such as a scamper round the park at the end of it. If the only time a puppy goes in the car is to visit the vet, it is not surprising that he views cars with some degree of suspicion. Once several excursions have been made without the puppy being sick, he will cease to distrust the car and your only trouble may be going somewhere without his wanting to come along.

The earlier in the day you can collect the puppy, the better for all. He will need time to get used to his new home before the light is turned out, especially as he is expected to settle down for his first night completely alone. If you can arrange to collect him early in the day, the breeder can make sure that he has not had any breakfast. The puppy will then have all day with you to play in the garden, explore his territory, have several naps and, hopefully, eat some of his prescribed meals. I say hopefully as some puppies can go off their food for a day or two. Provided that he starts to eat normally within a couple of days there is nothing to worry about, though you should make sure that he drinks some water so that he does not become dehydrated. If he is off his food, it is advisable to add some glucose to his water. If you have given him this opportunity to settle, when the time comes to leave him alone he should be relaxed and free from worry, and your chances of a relatively peaceful night will have been greatly increased.

The First Days

There are many ways to make that first night for the puppy less frightening. During the day you should have introduced him to his basket, or wherever he is expected to sleep, so that his bed smells familiar and friendly. If you have bought the basket with room for the puppy to grow, then make a comfortable nest at one end. Remember that he is not used to sleeping alone. I have heard it suggested that a hot-water bottle under the blanket and/or a ticking clock can help to settle a puppy and I do not doubt it is true, but chewing the rubber bottle and playing havoc with the clock might seem to him to be a lot more fun than going to sleep once he has been left alone.

Do make sure that he has relieved himself before you expect him to settle. His dam will have brought him up not to be dirty in the kennel and he will usually whine if he is uncomfortable and not sure where to go. If the breeder has used newspaper, several sheets near the door will encourage him to use that area. Puppies, like babies, are fairly predictable in their habits, and they need to be taken out as soon as they wake up from a nap and after feeding or a boisterous game. Whippets are clean little dogs and are rarely much trouble to house-train, but accidents are bound to happen with any puppy and you must be prepared to accept this.

Some owners let the puppy sleep in their room in his basket for a few nights until he is thoroughly settled, and I have to admit that this usually works well. The puppy can be moved to the kitchen after a couple of nights with very little trouble. However, if you let him sleep in your room for too long – say a week or so – you may have difficulty persuading him that the kitchen is an acceptable alternative. 'Start as you mean to go on' is a sensible maxim in training all puppies, and if you can face the prospect of one night of whines and scratches, firmly put the puppy to sleep where you want him to stay and be prepared for a disturbed night spent soothing him.

House Rules

If you do not want the puppy on the furniture or beds, you must be firm about this from the very beginning and provide him with somewhere that is his own. Some owners never allow the dogs upstairs for example, while others do not allow dogs on the furniture or beds. If the puppy is not to settle himself into your favourite chair, he must

Whippets like cages, and this type of cage will prove a worthwhile investment.

have a basket in the sitting room, somewhere warm and out of draughts. Whippets do not consider the floor – even when luxuriously carpeted – to be a suitable place to sleep. A fur rug in front of an open fire might be the only possible exception. So if you want to keep the chairs free of all dog hairs, a firm rule must be established from day one, and a place of his own provided. While he is very young, he will settle much better if his basket is next to your chair, so that you can put a hand down to stroke and reassure him frequently. Once he is more confident and at home, he may prefer a quiet corner next to the radiator or fire. The polystyrene-filled beanbag type of bed is greatly appreciated by Whippets, but should not be considered until the puppy is past all chewing stages. I once came home to a kitchen filled with polystyrene beads so I speak from experience. It took hours with a borrowed commercial vacuum cleaner to get rid of them, and even then I found small white beads in odd corners for months.

The best investment you can make to facilitate all areas of training your puppy is a proper crate or cage. A collapsible wire cage, large enough for him to stand, turn and lie down in comfortably as an adult dog, will mean that as a puppy he can be put to sleep in it overnight, with his bed at the back and lots of newspapers in front so there is no mess in the kitchen in the morning. He can be left in it with a bone and his toys while you are out for an hour shopping, and if you go to stay with friends or spend a night in a hotel, he can be put in his cage where he can do no damage and where he feels safe and at home. I have always found that Whippets like cages and will sleep there from choice, particularly if there is a blanket over it so that it seems like a little den, and it is in a warm quiet place, free from draughts.

Whippet puppies are very playful and can be destructive if left unsupervised in a room full of temptations. A box of toys in a corner of the kitchen will often avoid the systematic emptying of an open kitchen cupboard or waste-paper basket. A puppy thoroughly enjoys removing his rubber bones, balls, 'legal' slippers, pieces of old fur and so on from the box and carrying them around until they lose their attraction; whereupon he will go back for the next item, leaving the discarded toy in the middle of the floor. A toy box is also a very good way of training the pup to differentiate between those playthings that are permissible and those that are not.

Diet

The breeder should always provide you with a diet sheet for your new puppy and it is best to keep strictly to this for a week or so. The fewer things that change, the better for a youngster – leaving his first home and learning your ways is enough to cope with at first. As I said before, it may take a few days before the pup is eating well and finishing all his meals. When he gets to the stage of clearing the dish at mealtimes, you can start to make every meal a little larger. If he leaves some, cut down until he is finishing everything again. At nine weeks, Whippets should still be on five meals a day, but some will be ready to cut down to four and they should continue to be fed four small meals a day for some weeks. The next meal to be cut out – usually when the dog shows no interest in it – is the midday meal. Throughout their adult lives, most Whippets do much better on two small meals a day rather than one large one.

The following diet sheets are merely guidelines. Every breeder has his own methods of rearing and feeding, and the only thing that matters is whether the puppies are healthy and strong.

Typical Diet Sheet for Eight-Week-Old Puppy

7.30 a.m. Large tablespoon of top-quality tinned puppy food. Small handful of small mixer biscuit designed to be used with tinned food.

12.00 p.m. 2oz (57g) fish cooked in milk with rice, or
1 scrambled egg with rusk, or
2oz (57g) cooked chicken with vegetables and rice.

4.00 p.m. Bowl of milk (goat's or powdered puppy milk).
Rusks or few hard biscuits.

6.30 p.m. 3oz (85g) raw minced beef or minced tripe or cooked ox-cheek mixed with a handful of dampened puppy meal, preferably wholemeal. The biscuit should be damp but not soaked and of the best quality.

10.30 p.m. Bowl of cereal, porridge or biscuit, made with powdered puppy milk and sweetened with honey.

A vitamin supplement should be added to the fish and meat meals, though not to the tinned food as this is already vitaminized. Safe marrow bones and chews help with teeth.

If they finish their food, offer a little more next time; if they leave some, give less. If the puppy develops a runny tummy, cut out red meat and feed fish and rice or chicken and rice. The usual cause is too rich a diet with not enough carbohydrate.

The above is the diet sheet I give out with my puppies but I always stress that there are many other possibilities and that it is a suggested diet and no more. There are many excellent complete feeds on the market, many specially formulated for growing puppies and most of them suitable for Whippets. There is absolutely no reason why the puppy cannot be moved gradually on to a diet that is less time-consuming and expensive for the owner and continue to thrive. However, any change of diet should be made gradually to avoid tummy upsets. It is best to substitute one thing at a time until the new regime is complete.

By the time the puppy is twelve weeks old, he should be able to cope well with being fed four times a day. One of the main meals can be a commercially prepared complete food or tinned meat and mixer, but the other should be fresh meat or fish and good-quality biscuit meal. The other two meals should be milk and cereal.

Typical Diet Sheet for Twelve-Week-Old Puppy

7.30 a.m. 4oz (112g) good-quality tinned meat and mixer biscuit or complete food, prepared according to the manufacturer's instructions for age and weight of puppy, or scrambled eggs and rusks (twice a week).

12.00 p.m. Bowl of goat's milk or powdered puppy milk and several hard biscuits or rusks.

5.30 p.m. 4–5oz (112–140g) raw mince or minced tripe or cooked fish or cooked ox cheek. Dampened puppy meal. Rice or pasta make a change from biscuit meal.

10.00 p.m. Bowl of instant porridge or cereal made with warm milk and sweetened with a little honey.

Keep up the vitamin supplements as before but read the manufacturer's suggested dosage on the side of the tin and avoid overdoing the vitamins. Far from helping the development of your puppy you will upset the balance of his diet and can do quite serious damage.

By the time the puppy is six months old, he no longer needs the midday milk, and breakfast can be made smaller with a corresponding increase in the evening meal. He should be finishing all his food, but should still look nicely rounded and plump though not fat. Whippets do not finish growing until they are about ten months old and, depending on the line from which they are descended, their height can creep up until they are over a year old. Coursing height certificates are not granted until the dog is over two years old and all second-season dogs have to be remeasured before being granted a permanent certificate. It therefore follows that the diet of the young Whippet must take this slow maturation process into account if the puppy is to reach full potential.

Inoculations

Soon after you have collected your puppy, he will need inoculations to protect him against the various dog diseases. Depending upon his age and the area in which you live, these inoculations can be given from nine weeks onwards. If you can keep the puppy in your own garden and not let him come into contact with other dogs, it is perfectly reasonable to leave them until twelve weeks. He will be carrying anti-bodies from his dam, which should give him a certain amount of protection until then.

Your vet is the best person to advise you on when to inoculate, and whether it is safe to leave it until a little later. Dog puppies can react badly to the trauma of visits to the vet and might draw up one or both their testicles in protest. This will usually correct itself later but is a risk to be avoided if possible. It is also worth considering the point that the surgery is an excellent place to pick up infection. Always carry the puppy and never put him down on the floor or let him play with another dog in the waiting room. Only when the course of injections has been completed should you allow the puppy to romp with any other dogs except your own.

These inoculations, which normally offer the puppy excellent protection against distemper, leptospirosis, hepatitis and parvo-virus, will need to be boosted from time to time throughout his life. The certificate you will be given by the vet will tell you when boosters are due. The certificates also state when diseases are covered by that particular make of injection. If you move house and change vet, he will need to see the original certificate to check type and date of previous inoculations.

Grooming

Whippets have short, fine coats that look immaculate with very little effort on the part of the owner, but a quick groom with a rubber brush every day or so will ensure that as little hair as possible is shed onto furniture and clothing. Like all dogs, Whippets have a moulting season – spring and autumn – when their hair will come out far more profusely than normal and a daily groom will keep this under control.

This grooming time should be a pleasurable experience for the puppy, and is an excellent time to get him used to being handled and to check his coat for bramble thorns and any other debris. If he is destined for the show ring, asking him to stand on the table quietly without fidgeting while you check his teeth and stroke him gently is the best training he can have. Do make sure, however, that you stand him on a non-slip surface. Many a puppy has had his confidence shaken by sliding off a slippery table top, and it may take some time to reassure him.

Once every three weeks or so, many Whippets need their toenails clipped. This need varies with each dog and does not always depend on how much road walking they do. Some dogs need their claws clipped more often than others, but it is a very simple job with a proper pair of guillotine-type clippers with a sliding blade. It should not necessitate a visit to the vet once you feel sufficiently confident about tackling the task yourself. The nails should be cut to about an eighth of an inch (3mm) of the quick, which is easy to see in a white nail but impossible with black ones. If in doubt, err on the side of leaving too much, but by keeping the nails short you will ensure that the puppy's feet get the best chance to develop correctly. Long nails encourage the puppy to flatten his feet in order to walk comfortably, thereby inhibiting the development of good strong pads.

Warmth

Because of his fine coat, your Whippet will need a warm coat for winter walks when he is an adult, but as a puppy he will be growing too fast to justify the outlay on a new coat every few weeks. A knitted 'ganzy' or jersey will keep him warm if out in the car, but he should not be out on long walks much before six months, at which stage he will have grown enough to fit a coat. Playing and running in the garden or park, with a very short walk on the lead on the road, is all a young Whippet needs for exercise and, while playing, he will not want the encumbrance of a coat. He should never be allowed to get too cold or wet or he will lose condition and weight. A cold Whippet is a miserable animal, and is one of the reasons why the breed make much better house dogs than kennel dogs.

Training

Puppies, even those who are not going to be shown, need to be taught to stand sensibly for grooming and, equally, they all enjoy a game of chasing. A piece of fur tied on the end of a length of rope and swung on a long pole provides much good exercise and is very good training for those who will be chasing a lure in adulthood. Once again, do not overplay the game. It should be fun and provide excitement without exhausting the puppy.

He will also need to be taught to walk sensibly on a collar and lead, and you will need to proceed with lead training carefully if you are not to frighten him. Certainly, the first few times you attempt to walk him on a lead you will be astonished at what a good imitation of a bucking bronco can be given by a ten-week-old Whippet. Either that or he will sit down solidly and totally refuse to move at all. Start by putting a light collar on for a few minutes at a time, lengthening the period of wear day by day, until he forgets about the collar and plays about quite happily. Then put on the lead and ask him to come with you. Tempt him forward with a titbit if necessary, though you must make it quite clear that he must do as you want, and praise him when he trots even a few steps in the right direction. In a few days, if you have been firm and patient, he will have got the idea and will come quite willingly.

Apart from general training, it is unnecessary and even unwise to teach a young puppy much more until you have decided what his future holds. A show Whippet should not be taught to sit by pressure on his hindquarters for he will then sit in the show ring when the judge is examining him. A puppy intended for racing only should not be shown live quarry, as later on you will be asking him to be enthusiastic about chasing a piece of rag. By training him to behave sensibly in the house and on the lead, not to be afraid of the car, to stand still when you want to groom him, and by introducing him to the fun to be had chasing things, you are merely equipping him to be a Whippet.

4

Adult Management

Housing

There is always controversy within the Whippet world as to whether it is better to keep your dogs in kennels or in the house. Those who keep their dogs in the house are adamant that Whippets are only happy inside, and those who keep their dogs kennelled are equally certain that they perform better in the show ring and in the field if kept outside.

As with most other things in life, it is possible to compromise. My dogs sleep outside in heated kennels, with large grass runs. The kennels all have flaps, so that the dogs may go in and out whenever they wish. After the afternoon walk, they all come in and lie by the fire or, I am ashamed to say, on the chairs and they stay in, except to be fed, until we go to bed. This means that they are used to being in their

A basket in the sun is always appreciated.

51

Sitting on the sofa on top of a friend can also be very comfortable.

kennels for long periods, so on show days or coursing days they can be left without becoming distressed. It also ensures that they have excellent house manners, and receive the love, attention and contact with humans they need.

You must make the arrangements that suit you and your circumstances, as the needs of someone like myself with a kennel full of dogs, and those of a family with one or two pets are not necessarily the same. By sleeping the dogs outside, you may indeed be saving on wear and tear in the house, and on the housework produced by dog hairs and pawmarks, but you are also creating another area which has to be cleaned, heated and generally looked after.

A word of warning to anyone taking on an older puppy or adult. A Whippet who has been reared in a kennel, will take to life as a house dog very happily, but a Whippet who has been brought up and lived entirely in the house will not transfer easily to a kennel situation, and could become very distressed.

If your Whippet is going to be a house dog, he must know from an early age where his bed is, so that when you say 'Get in your basket', he does so instantly. The bed should be his base, and as such should be a permanent fixture. It should be in a warm, draught-free place, out of your way and provide the dog with somewhere quiet to sleep when everyone is too busy to pay him any attention. If he is to sleep in the kitchen at night, and that is where you would want him to go when visitors are around or he has just returned from a muddy walk, he will need a bed there but it is sensible to have a second bed for him in the living room where he can lie when he wants to be with the family. Whippets are affectionate dogs and need close human company if they are to thrive.

They are not as delicate as they might appear and can be housed outside if that is what suits the family. However, it would be cruel to expect a single Whippet, kept as a family pet, to sleep alone outside, and if you only want one dog and want to keep him under these conditions, do not have a Whippet. Given canine company, he will take quite happily to sleeping outside if he is accustomed to doing so from puppyhood and if he is provided with comfortable quarters.

Since Whippets have thin, fine coats and are susceptible to cold, they must be provided with weatherproof accommodation, free from draughts and with plenty of light if they are to be kept outside. The beds must be raised off the floor and have high sides, both to keep the bedding from falling out and to make sure no draughts affect the dogs. In cold weather they must have heat, though how much depends on the bedding provided. Many breeders use the red heat lamps used on pig and poultry farms, but the heaters with solid bulbs are safer. It is possible to obtain bulbs of different strengths for these lamps so they can be adjusted to suit the weather. Two dogs with deep bedding of shredded paper in a properly constructed bed will not need the same degree of heat as those bedded down on blankets. Insulating kennels will save on fuel bills and is well worth the initial outlay.

Kennels and runs have to be looked after and kept scrupulously clean to avoid disease. The sleeping area should be cleared and swept out once a week and sprayed with disinfectant. Some disinfectants are too strong for use in kennels and could cause irritation to the eyes and skin of the dogs so use one of the types specifically produced for use in kennels. All bedding should be inspected and changed regularly whether the dogs live in or out. Kennel runs also have to be kept spotless. The faeces should be cleared up morning and evening and, if there are concrete runs, they will need to be rinsed down with disinfectant and swept several times a week, daily if you have several dogs or are rearing a litter of puppies.

Feeding the Adult Dog

It is important to establish a routine when feeding your Whippet. Mealtimes are one of the main highlights of a dog's day and though how often you feed will depend on the dog, when you feed is up to you. For the sake of his general well-being it is as well to keep to a routine as far as possible.

By the time your Whippet is twelve months old he should be down to one main meal and one small meal a day, but some puppies that come from slow-maturing lines will need two more substantial meals a day until eighteen months or even all their lives. A small light breakfast, with the main meal late afternoon or early evening, and a couple of hard biscuits to take to bed are probably ideal for the majority of Whippets, but whichever method you adopt, the overall amounts you feed should not vary.

Two meals a day should not necessarily mean twice as much. If you want to know whether you are feeding correctly, look at the dog. If what greets you is a Whippet with bright eyes, shiny coat and cold nose, allied to a lively disposition and a svelte and streamlined figure, you cannot be going too far wrong.

A fat dog of any breed is a sad sight, and a fat Whippet looks worse than most. Most Whippets are not greedy by nature and will not normally gorge themselves meal after meal and day after day, but it is the instinct of wild animals to eat as much as they can whenever they can, as they are never sure when they might find their next meal. This instinct is still active in the domestic dog, including some Whippets, and it is up to you to maintain the correct level of nutrition to ensure a long, healthy and active life.

So what does the dog need for his continuing good health? The answer is that he should be given a diet that contains proteins, carbohydrates, fats and minerals in the correct proportion and balance. In the wild, the hunting dog eats all of his prey, not just the most tender pieces of flesh, and is thus provided with everything he needs for a balanced diet. If a pair of Whippets catch and kill a rabbit, they will either carry it back to you or, if they are hungry, they will settle down and devour the animal completely, fur, bones, and innards, and this is the natural way for them to behave. They are instinctively providing themselves with a perfectly balanced meal.

Proteins are necessary for the growth and maintenance of the working parts of the body: muscle, flesh, blood and bones. In a predominantly carnivorous animal, the main source of protein is meat, both the flesh of the animal and the offal. The offal consists of the liver, kidneys, heart, tripe and such. Beef has a higher food value than lamb or mutton, and horsemeat is richer in protein and mineral salts than either. By feeding both flesh and offal, many of the essential vitamins are provided. Meat also contains fats and mineral salts, such as iron salts, important for the blood; and calcium, which is essential for healthy bone development. Fish also has a high protein content and forms a highly acceptable alternative meal.

A wild dog would obtain most of the carbohydrate needed for producing energy and warmth by devouring the intestines of his prey. These also provide him with the necessary vitamins. A domestic dog obtains his carbohydrate intake from the farinaceous foods in his diet. To be digested by the dog, cereals have to be cooked and fed in the form of biscuits and meal, and from this part of his diet the animal also derives the bulk and roughage essential to keep his digestive system in good working order.

The vitamins necessary for the domestic dog include A, B, C, D and E. Vitamin A, which promotes tissue formation, is found mainly in dairy products, such as milk and butter, in cod-liver oil, green vegetables, peas, beans and spinach. Lack of vitamin A can retard growth. A lack of vitamin B tends to impair appetite and digestion. The usual sources of this vitamin are cereals, peas, beans, raw fruit, spinach, egg yolk, yeast and honey. Vitamin C is good for the condition of skin and joints, and a deficiency of vitamin C often leads to a loss of weight. Green foods, raw fruit, milk and liver are all sources of vitamin C.

The function of vitamin D is slightly different, and this vitamin can in fact be dangerous, in that overdosing can have an equally adverse effect on the dog. Vitamin D controls calcium equilibrium and regulates mineral metabolism, and a lack of this vitamin can cause rickets, deformity of the bones and general muscular weakness. The main source is sunshine, but it is present in cod-liver oil, egg yolk, milk and spinach.

A deficiency of vitamin E can cause loss of fertility in both male and female dogs. It helps in promoting good muscular development and tone. It is present in wheat, milk, lettuce and watercress.

As you can see from the above, the essential vitamins are present in food you would expect to feed your dog and, if you are giving him a variety of foods, or using a top-quality commercial diet, it is highly unlikely that he needs any more vitamins. Overdosing with vitamins can be just as dangerous as providing too meagre a diet and could, oddly enough, lead to the same result. The average adult Whippet, fed on a varied diet of meat, fish and wheatmeal biscuit, does not need a supplement. The only exception might be the addition of seaweed powder, which supplies minerals and trace elements possibly lacking in a normal diet. The dietary requirements of a bitch in whelp is discussed in Chapter 7, and the special needs of a racing Whippet are covered in Chapter 11.

Most breeders would consider that the best food for adult dogs is raw meat and tripe, fed with wheatmeal biscuit. Other offal, such as liver, heart and kidneys, should be cooked and should not constitute the sole meat fed as they lack many of the constituents of meat and tripe. They do, however, make a highly acceptable alternative from time to time.

It is true that some dogs do not like their meat uncooked, and some owners do not like handling quantities of raw meat, so by all means cook the meat for your dog if you prefer it. A few vegetables and an onion added to the pan will improve the smell while it is cooking. In the winter, you can add a handful of pearl barley to the casserole, and this makes a particularly welcoming meal for a tired dog at the end of a long, cold day's coursing.

However, I do not advise cooking green tripe and unless you are prepared to put up with the smell or feed the dog outside, you will not be able to use this cheap, nutritious and (to your dog) delicious form of protein. The purchase of green tripe for the dogs was forbidden by my husband until I obtained a small deep-freeze specially for dog food, but now that I can not only store it, but feed it outside, it is the main source of meat protein for my dogs.

Fish, chicken, rabbit and game such as hare make acceptable variations in the diet of a Whippet but if fed cooked, all of these require very careful sifting for bones, which is both time-consuming and messy. Because of this, they are not really suitable as a daily diet.

The meat should be mixed with the best-quality wheatmeal biscuits available. It is always advisable to buy a known, named brand as a lot of rubbish is sold in unmarked bags which often contain more than a reasonable amount of biscuit dust. The biscuit should be soaked, but not soggy. Warm water or the skimmed gravy from the cooked meat can be used, and ideally the biscuit should be dampened an hour before feeding. Many Whippets are extremely adept at removing the meat and leaving the biscuit, and for this reason it may be necessary to use the puppy grade of biscuit rather than the terrier size which might be considered more suitable for an adult Whippet, and to mix the meat and biscuit well before serving.

The general rule of thumb for the main meal is half a pound (200g) of meat a day per dog, mixed with 4 ounces (112g) of biscuit. Obviously the needs of each Whippet vary according to age, size, the amount of exercise taken and the metabolism of the individual. Some larger, younger or more active dogs will require more, while the more sedate ones will get too plump on this amount.

Breakfast should be a light snack rather than a meal. Scrambled egg and rusk; a raw egg beaten into a quarter of a pint (225ml) of milk; breakfast cereal and milk sweetened with a little honey or glucose; a handful of complete food in dry biscuit form; or some of the semi-moist commercial dog foods will all provide a nutritious beginning to your dog's day. If the dog looks thin on his prescribed ration, any extra needed could be given at breakfast.

Feeding the 'poor doer' this way makes sure that it is the dog who needs the extra that actually eats it, rather than his companion who whips in and removes the best bits while your attention is elsewhere. We once had a bitch who would bark loudly as soon as all the food bowls were down, and while all the others rushed to the door to see who was arriving, she would make a rapid inspection of everyone's bowl and snatch any particularly succulent morsel.

If feeding several dogs, it is always wise to have a strict routine. The dogs should be fed in the same order and in the same spot on the floor every time, and a careful eye kept that no one emulates the old rascal described above and steals another's titbits. Saying each dog's name as you set down each bowl reinforces the routine.

On being put to bed for the night, a couple of hard biscuits completes the diet and helps soften the blow of being left alone for eight hours. In Whippet Heaven you sleep on the bed under the duvet every night, and eight hours out in the kennel or in a basket in the kitchen can seem a long time without human company.

I am feeding a number of dogs, most of whom are working – either showing or running, some doing both – and I am therefore prepared to go to some considerable trouble to keep them in top condition. I feed a varied diet of raw green tripe and wholemeal biscuit, fish and rice, cooked ox cheek and vegetables, and use commercially prepared foods, such as tinned meat and mixer or complete food and gravy for a quick, light breakfast.

Seaweed powder is added to all the main meals, otherwise no additives are given except for bitches who are in whelp or lactating, puppies, saplings and the very elderly. All the dogs have access to grass in their run and in the garden and they all eat the coarse couch grass from time to time. Some are more compulsive grazers than others and why dogs have this need is not certain. However, with this habit in mind, it is as well to be careful with the weedkillers and pesticides used in your garden.

In a busy household with one or two pet dogs, it would be unrealistic to expect owners to spend this amount of time controlling the diet of their Whippets, but the principle of a varied diet based on meat and biscuitmeal remains unchanged. Commercial dog-food companies employ highly qualified dieticians to ensure that their products will provide a dog with a balanced diet, and it is undoubtedly true that many dogs do very well fed entirely on tinned food or complete feeds of one sort or another. The choice provided by commercially prepared foods is enormous, the quality of the best ones beyond doubt, but I cannot help but feel that fresh food is preferable, both for humans and dogs.

Tinned or dried food has a place but should not dominate the diet. If you opt for ease of management by using dried complete food to which water or gravy is added, tinned meat and mixer biscuit and complete food in expanded biscuit form, you should still be able to provide variety and interest in the diet.

All dogs should have a permanent supply of clean drinking water. Water bowls should be rinsed and wiped every day. This is particularly necessary for dogs fed any appreciable amount of the semi-moist or dry complete foods. It is absolutely essential that water is available whenever they need it, or permanent kidney damage can result. There are manufacturers' warnings about the need for water with all these foods, but it is surprising how many owners disregard them.

5

General Health and Welfare

This does not set out to be a book on canine veterinary matters, but anyone with the responsibility of caring for stock of some kind needs to know something about the animal in their care. There is nothing difficult or mysterious about looking after Whippets, or any other dog for that matter. Common sense, together with a basic feel for the well-being of your animals is all that is needed. It is not a mystic art denied to all but the few, but if you were not born with stock-sense nor brought up amongst animals, it may take a little longer to learn. Time and experience should teach you to know at a glance if your Whippet is feeling on top of his form or is slightly off-colour, even with no specific symptoms to point the way, but he cannot tell you – you have to see for yourself.

Whippets, as a breed, are normally very healthy and are free from most of the inherited diseases that affect many pedigree dogs. Most visits to the vet, apart from routine booster inoculations, will be as a result of an injury sustained while in full pursuit of a rabbit or squirrel, rather than any illness. However, by keeping a careful eye on the behaviour of your Whippet you can often forestall serious trouble. Your Whippet should greet you in the morning with enthusiasm, and if he appears anything other than full of life, there must be a reason.

The Grooming Session

The grooming session is the best time to take a special look at your dog. As well as going over the Whippet with a rubber-bristled brush and finishing with a polish from a soft cloth, it is a very good idea to run your hands over his body as you will be able to feel any little thorns left in the skin. In fact, a good hand massage is one of the best ways of getting a dog really fit, as any Greyhound trainer will tell you. A ten-minute hand massage using embrocation is part of basic conditioning for racing and coursing Whippets, serving to tone up the

59

muscles and keep the skin clear of parasites. This is also the time to check the eyes for any sign of discharge, see that ears are clean, the nose cold and damp and the coat glossy.

During the grooming session, have a look at the length of the dog's nails. It is much easier to snip a little off regularly than it is to leave this job until the nails are very long and causing trouble. As mentioned previously, the guillotine-type of nail clippers are easy to manage. If you do a lot of road walking during very hot weather you may find tar sticking to the fur around the dog's feet or between the toes. This must be removed as it can cause nasty sores. Cotton wool dampened with methylated spirit will get rid of the tar quite easily.

Open the dog's mouth and have a look at his teeth and gums. Some dogs are blessed with teeth that remain white and free from plaque until they are quite elderly, while others, fed on exactly the same diet and with the same access to marrow bones and hard biscuit, need the ministrations of a soft toothbrush and toothpaste from quite an early age. There is even a special powdered toothpaste for dogs if he does not like the taste of your favourite brand! A brush every fortnight will

Whippets need their nails cutting regularly.

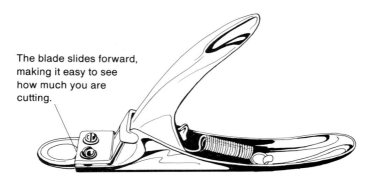

The blade slides forward, making it easy to see how much you are cutting.

Sliding nail clippers.

keep the teeth gleaming, but you may need to do this more often as the dog gets older. Gums should be a healthy pink; if they are very pale it may be a sign of anaemia and a visit to the vet is called for.

The ears of a Whippet are fine and silky. If the edges of the ear become dry it may be because he lacks a little oil in his diet, and a dessertspoonful of corn oil added to his food will prevent this. Rubbing some baby oil into the edges of the ear will get rid of the roughness (cod-liver oil is even better if you can stand the smell).

The inside of the ear should be clean and free from dirt and wax. A small amount of dirt can be removed with a cottonwool bud and baby oil, but if there is an unpleasant smell, or if the wax persists, then once again you will need your vet to ensure that no parasites are present deep down in the ear. Never poke or prod deep into the ear in an effort to clean – the dog will yelp and leap about and you could do untold damage.

The nose should be cold and damp and free from discharge. A hot dry nose can be the forerunner of various dog diseases, as can any nasal discharge. The hot dry nose can also mean that he has been sound asleep buried under his blanket next to the stove for the last hour, so a careful eye rather than instant panic is called for. A nasal discharge is another matter and if persistent, or allied to other symptoms, should be tended to immediately by a vet.

Another important guide to the health of the dog is the colour, size and firmness of his faeces. These will be affected by his diet. A mainly meat diet will produce smaller, harder motions, but the cereal-based complete foods will produce more copious, moist ones. If the dog has been eating bones, the faeces may be hard and white, but generally speaking they should be firm and any sign of looseness should be watched carefully. If the dog appears otherwise well, but is passing very loose motions, remove all red meat from the diet for two days and feed white meat or fish and rice instead. Diarrhoea should not be allowed to go unchecked for any longer, and if the change of diet has not worked, then nothing but water and glucose to drink and a trip to the vet are essential.

Kennel Cough

One symptom to watch, or rather listen for, is a dry, persistent cough. Isolate the dog immediately and notice how often he coughs. He may merely have swallowed something that has scratched his throat, but he may be developing kennel cough.

There seem to be as many strains of kennel cough as there are dogs and it is very difficult to inoculate against this disease. Normally it is annoying rather than dangerous but it spreads through a kennel like wildfire. The infection can be carried from one dog to another by tiny droplets on the ground where a dog has coughed. Some dogs can develop it very badly and cough for weeks, causing their owners and themselves considerable distress.

It is very important that dogs with kennel cough are kept as quiet as possible; violent exercise, such as free running and galloping, can leave them with a weakened heart. If your dog has a dry persistent cough and you suspect that he has picked up this infuriating illness, ring your vet before you take the animal to the surgery. He may prefer to give you an appointment so that your dog does not infect other animals in the waiting room.

Kennel cough is very infectious and can take three weeks to develop, so if one of your dogs is coughing, all other dogs on your premises must be isolated until three weeks after the coughing has ceased. They should not mix with other dogs until this period is over, and only then can you consider yourself free to attend shows, go racing or participate in any other dog activity.

If you are worried about your dog – if he is shivering, his coat is standing up and he is generally off-colour – it is very easy to take his temperature. A healthy dog's temperature is between 100.9 and 101.7 °F) (38.3 and 38.7 °C). If it is normal, it will serve to reassure you and if not, it will help the vet in his diagnosis. Do not take the temperature immediately after exercise, when the body temperature can be expected to be higher than normal. You should use a rectal thermometer which has been lubricated with a little oil or vaseline. If possible, get someone to hold the dog, then raising his tail insert the thermometer at a slightly upward angle. Hold it in for a full minute, remove and wipe with a tissue before reading it.

Whippets are rarely ill but if the dog seems off-colour and is running a temperature, reach for the telephone and call your vet as soon as possible.

Your Vet

All the above makes it sound as if you will be spending a lot of time checking your dog and visiting the vet; but in fact it only takes a few moments each day to do the checking, and it is very rare indeed that you will have to take a Whippet to your vet. In my experience, trips to the surgery are either calm, organized visits for routine inoculations arranged well in advance, or emergency, weekend, out-of-hours visits for injuries, such as cuts caused by wire.

It is at times like these, when you are already distressed and worried by the injury, that you will learn to value a competent vet, and if you are fortunate enough to discover one who appreciates Whippets, stick to him or her – their worth is above rubies. Running a good veterinary practice is expensive, however, and you must expect to pay for expert care and attention and for the round-the-clock service you receive, so one of the pet insurance plans which are available nowadays is a sensible investment.

Injuries

Whippets put great strain on their legs and feet while running and are prone to minor injuries. With a little experience and common sense, many such injuries can be treated at home, saving your vet's time and your money. However, it cannot be stressed often enough that until you have some experience, or if you are in any doubt at all about the best treatment, take the dog to the vet.

Some experienced owners of working Whippets do not have small cuts stitched or attended by a qualified veterinary surgeon, but if you are a novice, it is probably better to be safe than sorry. A night spent licking a very minor cut can turn it into a large tear by morning, whereas two stitches would have ensured that the dog left the wound alone, allowing it to heal much quicker and leaving no unsightly scar. The saying that a stitch in time saves nine was probably started by the owner of a working Whippet!

At some time in their lives, most Whippets will suffer from minor injury to their feet or legs. Running at the speed they do and with the enthusiasm they bring to the chase, it is not surprising that from time to time they will bruise a toe, injure a nail or slightly sprain a leg, and although there may be no obvious injury, the dog appears lame. Examine the offending limb carefully from toe-nail to elbow, bending and moving the joints gently.

Sometimes there is a swelling at the point of injury, sometimes the dog will wince with certain movements. If there is a soft swelling around a joint, the same remedy as you would give a sprained ankle in a human will work equally well with a Whippet. Ice packs applied as often as possible, a light supporting bandage and rest will reduce the swelling. The homoeopathic remedy of arnica 6 will help bring out the bruising and speed recovery. Give two of these tiny tablets every hour for six hours; thereafter two, three times a day, for three days.

If there is no swelling or heat in the leg, very gently pull the dog's leg out in front of him, bend it at the knee and push it back. If he winces or appears to resist, he may have pulled a muscle, in which case rest is the main ingredient for the cure with a light massage with embrocation, and again arnica 6 to bring out the bruising. If, after two days of rest and gentle massage the dog is still lame, take him to the vet.

A 'knocked-up' toe is fairly common with any running dog and unless you suspect that the toe is fractured, it does not really necessitate calling your vet. This injury occurs when the joints of the toe are pushed out of place, and even though the dislocation may be only temporary, the membrane around the joint will be damaged and fill with fluid. If it is not treated, this fluid will harden into fibrous tissue leaving the toe permanently swollen and perhaps stiff. Use bone radiol linament and follow the instructions on the bottle with care, as this type of linament is very strong and only intended for certain purposes.

The nail beds can also become sore with impacted mud and, if left, will become infected. Wash the feet thoroughly in warm water and antiseptic. Use a nail brush to dislodge the mud and dry thoroughly. Until the area of the nail bed is healed, a twice daily soaking in Epsom Salts and water is called for, and although this may be a tedious job, it is hardly expensive and may save you a vet's bill for treatment to an infected foot.

The most important ingredient of any of these cures, however, is rest, and you must not be tempted to let the dog off the lead until you are absolutely certain that he is completely sound. One very good way of being sure is to take him out on the lead on a gravel drive. Gravel seems to find all the sore places on a dog's foot, and if his feet are at all sensitive, wait another day or so.

Eyes

Whippets who live in the country or go hunting in brambles and undergrowth can sometimes get a grass seed or small thorn lodged in the eye. They will close the eye very firmly and refuse to let you investigate. As gently as possible, prise open a corner and drop in a soothing liquid, such as warm water and boracic powder or Optrex. Do this two or three times in an effort to dislodge the object, but if the eye remains shut, you will have to take the dog to the vet. On no account try to remove anything imbedded in the eye.

Basic Medicines

Even if you have only one Whippet and live in the city, it is certain that sooner or later you will need some basic medicines and equipment if you are not to waste both your vet's time and your money. These should include:

a rectal thermometer
nail clippers
round-nosed scissors
cotton wool
a roll of 2in (5cm) bandage (the self-adhesive stretch type obtainable
    from the vet is easier to apply)
a roll of 4in (10cm) bandage
a packet of non-stick sterile gauze
a roll of sticky tape
antiseptic dusting powder
antiseptic (always use well diluted)
antibiotic ointment
embrocation (for general hand massage)

bone radiol
Epsom salts
eye ointment and lotion
arnica 6 tablets (a herbal remedy for bruising)
arnica lotion (for massaging bruises and sprains)

Any other medicines, including worming preparations, should be obtained from, and used under, the direction of your vet. It is most important, both for the dog and for your family, that your dog is thoroughly wormed against both roundworms and tapeworms at least three times a year. The media are all too ready to blame dogs for cases of blindness in children caused by the *Toxocara canis* roundworm and, indeed, though rare, it is true that there are occasions when children have been blinded by the tiny worm present in the faeces of untreated dogs. It is vital therefore that all dogs are wormed regularly, and even if your dog never goes near a public park or has anything to do with children, he will be healthier for being rid of these parasites.

The Care of the Elderly Whippet

Whippets lead long and healthy lives, but they too grow old and need a little more care and attention if they are to end their days in comfort. They have given you unstinted love and devotion over the years, and it is up to you to repay some of this at the end of their lives. They will certainly need less food, but this should be of the very best quality and be divided into smaller, more frequent meals. A vitamin supplement should be added.

They should be allowed to take as much or as little exercise as they desire – only they know how stiff they are feeling each day.

An old dog, like an elderly person, feels the cold, and it may be necessary to provide him with a knitted coat at night, and no pensioner should be put out in a kennel. Whippets grow old very gracefully, and it is no hardship to find a warm, quiet corner where he can be near you when the youngsters in the kennel or kitchen become too much for him.

Euthanasia

Finally, it is the responsibility of the owner to make sure that his old dog does not suffer. If he has had a severe heart attack, or is in pain, then the decision to call the vet, while never easy, is the right thing to do. Senility, incontinence and confusion make it more difficult to know when that sad moment has arrived. It is tempting to put it off for one day and then another, but the welfare of the dog must be the prime consideration. You must not let your feelings allow you to keep him alive on drugs and pills because you cannot face your duty to an old and loved friend. Animals do not suffer from our fear of death and anticipation of the unknown, and pets have the right to a more humane end than that allotted to their counterparts in the wild.

If it is at all possible, do not take your dog to the surgery, but have your vet come to the house and, whatever happens, stay with him and hold him until the end. You will be surprised how gentle is the end.

When it is over, try not to think of your own unhappiness, but remember the years of pleasure you have had together. The best memorial to him will be your determination to have another Whippet.

6

Breeding

Before you consider the possibility of breeding from your bitch, there are certain very important questions which you should ask yourself. First of all, you must decide whether your girl is of sufficient quality to be used as a brood bitch. The fact that you love her and that she is a charming family pet is not really a good enough reason to increase the already over-populated canine world. Only bitches with a top-class pedigree, excellent temperament and with no serious breed faults should be considered for breeding purposes. It is a fallacy that bitches 'need' to have a litter and if you want a second Whippet, you would do much better to go back to the breeder from whom you obtained your pet and ask them to let you know when they have another puppy of similar breeding. If your bitch has been kept in good condition and you have provided a kind and loving home, they will be only too delighted to find you a companion for her. Good pet homes are greatly prized and appreciated by responsible breeders, who care very much what happens to all their puppies.

It is this responsibility for the puppies which lies at the bottom of the warning to take care and be very sure before embarking on breeding. You should have the proper facilities to rear the litter.

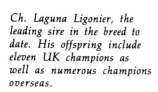
Ch. Laguna Ligonier, the leading sire in the breed to date. His offspring include eleven UK champions as well as numerous champions overseas.

Ch. Deepridge Mintmaster, a sire with considerable influence on the race-track as well as in the show ring.

Puppies need a happy and safe environment, with interesting things to see and do – have you this sort of space? Have you the time to play with and socialize them and the financial resources to feed them properly and cope with unexpected vet's bills? Rearing a healthy litter is an expensive business so it is pointless to mate your bitch with any idea of profit in mind.

You will also have to be prepared to help your puppy purchasers long after they have left you – even take a puppy back if something goes wrong. Whippets are not everyone's choice and it is not always easy to sell the puppies by nine or ten weeks. Sometimes it will be twelve weeks before suitable homes can be found. Can you cope with three or four boisterous three-month-old pups?

If you cannot in all honesty answer these questions in the affirmative, forget about breeding and content yourself with reaping the benefits of others' experience.

Choosing a Stud Dog

However, it may be that you have all the facilities. If you are a novice, it is better to have someone advise and help you. Perhaps you do have a beautifully bred bitch whose offspring will be a credit to her and the breed, and whose success in some area of Whippet activity justifies a litter. In this case, you must set about finding a suitable sire for her puppies. Without a doubt, the best person to advise you on this would be the breeder of the bitch, but advice is all they can give you – the ultimate decision will rest with you.

If you have been exhibiting, and it is your bitch's success in the show ring that has encouraged you to breed from her, you will already have a picture in your mind of the type of puppies you are hoping for. You will have seen many potential sires amongst the winning dogs in the ring and you will have read and studied the Kennel Club Standard for the breed until it is engraved on your heart.

You should be aware of your bitch's good points and her faults, so that you can choose a dog to complement or offset these faults. The obvious choice would appear to be a top-winning dog from the same blood-lines as your bitch, preferably one whose progeny are already being shown and who exemplify the type and quality you seek.

Once again, advice may be needed, for you will want to assess not only the phenotype of the potential sire (that is, the traits that you can see by looking at the dog), but also his genotype (the genetic make-up of the individual contained in his pedigree). The old saying, 'what is bred in the bone, will out in the flesh' is only too true where dogs are concerned.

It is sensible to obtain the pedigrees of the stud dogs you have short-listed and study them carefully. The owners of stud dogs are quite used to being asked for pedigrees and will supply them happily, though it is just as well to make sure that they understand you are just doing some careful research and not making a commitment to use their dog.

Much has been written on the subject of in-breeding, line-breeding and outcrossing. Generally speaking, line-breeding may be defined as the mating of cousins and distant relatives. In-breeding is the mating of much closer relations: brother to sister, father to daughter, mother to son. In-breeding should be left to the real experts who have the knowledge to interpret pedigrees and who are familiar with the ancestry of the animals named.

This also applies to outcrossing, that is the breeding of animals with no relationship to each other for at least five generations. By outcrossing your bitch, even to a well-known stud, you could be bringing in some very undesirable traits, and will not increase your chances of reproducing the best qualities of either parent. That is not to say that some outcross litters are not successful, but you are hardly stacking the deck in your own favour, and it certainly makes the assessing of future litters more difficult.

It is of course essential to outcross from time to time within a breeding programme to increase the genetic pool but, again, a knowledge of pedigrees enables an experienced breeder to do this without losing type and without bringing in unwanted characteristics from other lines.

If you have been racing your bitch, much the same ideas will apply. You will want to choose the fastest and most courageous dog available, but if you can find one with some ancestry in common with your bitch, you will, by the laws of genetics, be increasing the possibility that the puppies will carry those genes that result in the speed and endurance you admire.

Responsible breeders have as their goal the production of sound, healthy dogs free from hereditary diseases and able to lead an active life. Reliable, friendly, outgoing temperaments are equally essential for dogs to live in the social environment of our time. There is a small, but vociferous minority, who would like to see dogs banned from our streets, parks, beaches and all public places, and it is as well to give these people nothing about which to complain. The media are always delighted to report any story about a 'savage' dog, though there is very little nationwide coverage for some of the horrific instances of Man's treatment of the dog.

Mating the Bitch

Breeders' opinions vary as to when to mate a bitch for the first time. Probably the ideal time is about eighteen months to two years, at her third or fourth season. If you do this, she can have her second or third litters much later, at five or six years of age. If you delay the first litter for too long, you may have difficulty in getting her into whelp for the first time.

However, a bitch should not be mated at her first season. She is much too young and immature herself and the drain on her resources may mean that she will never develop properly. Neither should she be mated on every successive season. It is a great strain on a bitch to rear a litter and she needs time to build up her strength between each one.

Once you have decided to mate your bitch, make sure that all her inoculations are up to date, so that the puppies have the maximum amount of antibodies when they are born. Worm her thoroughly before the expected time of her season, and again when she first comes in.

Having chosen a suitable stud dog, and agreed on the stud fee, do let the owner of the dog know roughly when your bitch is due in season. When she actually comes into season, confirm this immediately so that arrangements can be made to take the bitch to the dog for mating. Nothing is more frustrating than being telephoned the day before mating should take place and being expected to be available without notice.

It is one of the most infuriating facts of dog breeding that the most suitable dog inevitably lives at the other end of the United Kingdom, and you may have to travel some distance to achieve the ideal mating. It is also a fact of dog breeding that the right day for mating is either Christmas Day, New Year's Day, or your Wedding Anniversary!

When the bitch first comes into season, the vulva becomes swollen and the discharge is a dark red colour. After about ten to twelve days, ovulation occurs and the discharge fades to a clearer pale colour. The bitch will then be ready to accept the dog. This is what breeders mean when they ask if the bitch is still showing colour.

In general, Whippet bitches are ready about twelve to fourteen days after the first show of colour, but this varies from individual to individual, and it is possible that your bitch will not accept the dog until a day or so later than this. It is also possible that you missed the first signs of her season as Whippet bitches keep themselves very clean. It is as well to verify that she is ready before setting off on what may be a long journey: if you do not have a dog you can use to test her reactions, try running your hand down her back – if she twitches her tail and holds it to one side, she is probably ready to stand.

Some breeders like to have two matings, especially for a maiden bitch, or if the dog is untried. It is by no means essential, and for a proven dog or bitch, not even preferable. Much depends on the length of the 'tie', that is the time during which the dog and bitch remain locked together during mating. This is caused by a swelling at the base of the male organ and prevents his withdrawal for a time. The dog will usually dismount and prop his hind leg over the bitch so that they remain hindquarter to hindquarter until they are able to break free naturally.

Ch. Cottonmere Monty of Oakbark, a beautifully marked fawn and white parti-colour.

This can be anything from five to forty minutes, and care should be taken that the dog is not hurt during this time by the bitch trying to break away. The owner of the stud dog usually slips an arm around the hind legs of the couple, steadying and calming both animals. If there has been a good tie, it is unlikely that a second mating will be necessary. However, if the dog slips out within a minute or two, it would be as well to try again after resting them both.

Success in the show ring, or on the coursing field or race-track, is how a breeder's success is usually measured, but this method of measurement does not always reveal the temperament of the animal in his kennel. You should take some time and trouble, therefore, to get to know the stud dog and his owner, before making a final decision, as it is absolutely certain that most of your puppies will sell as pets to homes where the nature of the animal is of paramount importance.

Basic Genetics

A pedigree is more than just a list of names, champions and non-champions. It is a collection of genes – a gene pool – and it is how these genes come together which will determine how your puppies turn out. Genetics is the branch of biology which deals with descent, variation and heredity and, as such, a basic knowledge of the subject is essential to successful breeding, especially if you are going to breed more than a one-off litter and embark on a serious breeding programme.

There are many excellent books on genetics (*see* Bibliography on page 174). Most are very technical and demand concentrated study, but should be required reading for a serious breeder. It is not the intention here to do more than briefly glance at this subject to enable the reader to gain a basic understanding of the laws of heredity.

One of the most famous of the early genetic scientists was a Czechoslovakian monk who taught science in the local school. His name was Gregor Mendel, and he conducted his research into inherited characteristics in the 1860s. The term genetics would have been unknown to Mendel, and was not used until forty years later, when it was coined by William Bateson for what was then considered a new science.

Mendel did his experimentation with peas, observing such obvious differences as shape and colour. Dogs have thousands, rather than hundreds, of genes however, and it is therefore much more difficult to predict results with animals than it is with plants, although the same laws apply.

Mendel crossed pure red flowers with pure white ones and in the first generation all the resulting flowers were red. However, when he crossed the apparent red hybrids with each other, one flower in four was white, while the other three were red. What he learnt was that the white colour (the recessive) was not destroyed in the first cross – it was hidden. He called the red flowers dominant since they could be seen, and the white recessive since they were apparently suppressed. In the next generation, when the two hybrids were crossed (still apparently red, but carrying the white suppressed gene) the white showed clearly.

Dominants and Recessives

The way in which dominant and recessive genes work is further complicated by the fact that not all dominant genes are desirable and not all recessive are undesirable. It is generally agreed that dark eyes and a good mouth are dominant, but a good layback of shoulder and well-angulated stifles are recessive. Breeders are therefore constantly working to bring to the fore the desirable traits, some dominant and some recessive.

This is particularly so in the case of colour breeding. Not everyone wants a brindle Whippet, but the genes that produce this colour are very dominant and can, in the first generation, appear to overcome other colours. Black, on the other hand, is a recessive colour and it is virtually impossible to produce a good dense black coat unless there are the genes for black present on both sides of the pedigree. Even then, one of the parents must themselves be black. All this makes breeding for colour an area strictly for the dedicated experts – it is quite difficult enough to produce a top-class Whippet of any colour.

Many traits are not inherited from a single gene, but are the result of several genes coming together (polygenetic). The more genes carrying the desired traits there are present in both animals, the greater the chance of these traits appearing in the new individuals.

It is no good trying to correct a fault by combining two animals with extreme faults in order to obtain one with the correct conformation. If you mate a very large dog with a very small bitch you are likely to get very large or very small puppies. You are not creating new genes, only bringing together what is already in the pedigree. Even if you do get, more by chance than anything else, one of the correct size, it is not likely that the next generation will also be of a correct size.

Therefore it follows that if your bitch is, for example, over-angulated in hindquarters, what you should be looking for is a dog with correct angulation, i.e. one who carries the genes for correct angulation. This way, those puppies in your litter who take after the sire, and who are correct in angulation, will have every possibility of breeding true in future generations.

It is often said that a rather average bitch from a good pedigree, is preferable as a foundation bitch to a top-winning specimen with a thoroughly mixed pedigree, or one of unknown quality. This is because a bitch carries in her genetic pool all the possibilities of her ancestors, especially those within the last three generations. The bitch with the top-class line-bred pedigree will produce far more good puppies than the show-stopper of dubious ancestry, always provided that she herself is indeed of average quality, with no extreme faults.

Of course those traits that you can see (the phenotype) and study in the parent animals matter, but what is 'bred in the bone' (the genotype) is just as important.

7

Whelping

Care of the Bitch in Whelp

Having achieved a successful mating, how do you look after your valuable bitch? The answer is that you look after her exactly the same way you did before she was mated! She is not ill and, to begin with, she needs no extra food or vitamin supplements although you can give a raspberry leaf tablet twice a day from the day she is mated until five days after whelping. This homoeopathic remedy is said to clear the bloodstream and aid in an easy whelping.

She should be allowed normal exercise, though it would not be sensible to let her run with a pack of other dogs in case she gets banged or badly knocked.

By the time she is five weeks in whelp, it should be fairly obvious that the mating was successful. Her teats may be more prominent and her waistline somewhat thicker. She may also have gone off her food at about four weeks for a few days. Between the twenty-eighth and thirtieth day, your vet would be able to palpate her and probably confirm the pregnancy, and there is a new pregnancy test available which is diagnosed from two millilitres of blood, which is also said to be reliable. However, she either is or is not in whelp, and it is best to be patient and avoid upsetting her in any way at all with unnecessary visits to the vet.

Once you have decided that she is in whelp, a daily vitamin dose of calcium is recommended, while still continuing with the raspberry leaf tablets. In order to produce good strong puppies, the bitch must have enough calcium-phosphorous and vitamins. From six weeks onwards, she will need a gradually increased diet, with extra meat, fish and eggs, though it is better to give this in the form of an extra meal, rather than a greater amount for supper.

The latest research suggests that if you worm the bitch on the forty-second day of pregnancy with a suitable worming compound, you will catch most of the worm larvae which are migrating from her muscle tissue to the whelps. Such a compound should only be obtained from, and used under, the instruction of your vet.

Whelping

The normal period of gestation in canines is sixty-three days or nine weeks, though it is perfectly normal for bitches to whelp up to four days early. It is also normal for bitches to whelp a day or so late, but this is more worrying, and you should monitor the bitch very carefully if she is even a day late. I always move into the spare room with the bitch for the week before she is due, as puppies, like babies, seem to prefer to be born in the safety of the night.

Remind your vet that the bitch is due to whelp just in case any difficulties arise, and check that he will be prepared to remove the dewclaws at three or four days old. If he is one of those members of the profession who refuse to remove dewclaws on the grounds that it is 'mutilation', you had better find a new vet pretty quickly. Dewclaws can cause constant trouble with a Whippet and must be removed when the pups are about three days old. If done then, it is a quick, virtually painless operation; later on, it will require an anaesthetic and stitching.

The normal temperature of a healthy dog is between 100.9°F and 101.7°F (38.2 and 38.7°C) but several hours before she whelps, the bitch's temperature will drop as low as 97 or 98 °F (36.1 or 36.6 °C). Most bitches also refuse all food for between twelve and twenty-four hours before whelping.

The first outward signs that whelping is about to commence is that the bitch becomes very restless, and wanders around the house scratching in corners and totally ignoring the clean, carefully prepared whelping box placed in a suitably quiet spot for her convenience.Keep a careful eye on her and when she starts contractions persuade her to stay in her box. Do make sure that she is not disturbed at all during this time, neither by other dogs nor by people other than yourself. The first puppy should arrive within one or two hours of contractions starting and if at the end of this time, nothing has happened, contact your vet immediately.

The puppies are born encased in a membrane bag that the bitch will tear open with her teeth.How much you help during the whelping is a matter for debate, but if you are going to be of any assistance, you should have on hand a pair of scissors with blunt ends, a suitable disinfectant in which to keep them, plastic bags, clean soft towels for

*Whippet bitch a few hours before whelping. Notice how the puppies
have dropped and are now being carried very low ready for birth.
When let off her lead immediately after this photograph was taken,
Chantress went hunting in the woods for an hour and came back
very pleased with herself.*

drying the pups, kitchen paper, and a small cosy basket with a hot
water bottle under the blanket in which to put the clean, dry puppies
while their siblings are in the process of arriving.

If you allow the bitch to bite the umbilical cord, it is quite likely that
she will pull too hard, causing a small hernia. With sharp scissors, it is
very easy to cut the cord leaving about two inches (5 centimetres) and
causing no bleeding. If you intend, as you should, to keep careful
records, a pair of kitchen scales to weigh the pups, and pencil and paper
to jot down their markings and birth-weight will also be needed.

It is quite natural for the bitch to eat the afterbirth, and this contains
minerals and vitamins and will aid in the contractions. However, your
bitch is not going to have to go without food for many days while her
puppies are young, and so she has no need of this form of sustenance.
If she does eat all the afterbirths, she will have a very dark green

discharge for many days after the birth and very likely diarrhoea as well. So, if possible, remove all but the first of the afterbirths (hence the plastic bags). Take care in counting these as the retention of one can cause infection later, but never attempt to pull it out yourself. Often the birth of the next puppy will bring it out.

Sometimes a puppy will look as if it is dead on arrival but do not be too quick to pronounce it dead. Wrap it in a towel, massage it gently and open its mouth so that the bitch can lick inside and clear the air passages. If it is still not showing signs of life, hold it very firmly in the towel, supporting its head carefully and give one sharp downward shake in an effort to clear the air passages and start the breathing process.

The number of puppies born in a litter varies considerably, but it does seem to run in families. If your bitch was one of a litter of nine, it is highly likely that she too will produce large families, and you should be ready to cope with the extra work this entails and be in a position to home them all. Some bitches are more restrained and only have small litters of three or four, which makes life easier for all concerned, not least the bitch herself. It follows therefore that the average falls somewhere between the two extremes.

Caring for the Bitch and her Litter

When no further puppies have been born for an hour or so, and the bitch settles down and goes to sleep, it is likely that she has finished whelping. Remove all the debris, wash her quarters with warm water and dry her gently. Give her clean bedding and leave her in peace with her babies.

The thermal bedding now available is ideal for whelping bitches and rearing puppies, as it allows any moisture through on to the newspaper underneath but stays dry on the surface. This means the pups remain warm and the fur-like texture gives them a good grip for their tiny feet. It is also much more comfortable for the bitch who is going to spend a great deal of time during the next few weeks lying with her puppies. This bedding washes very easily in a washing machine, which makes your job of keeping mother and babies immaculately clean much easier.

When she has had a good rest, take the bitch outside so that she can relieve herself and offer her some milk and glucose. Later, she can have small meals of white meat or fish and rice with a calcium supplement and within a few days she will be eating normally. For a day or so, you may have to lift her off her puppies to take her outside. Whippet bitches are very devoted mothers and often do not want to leave the puppies even for a few moments.

Puppies start suckling very soon after being born, some trying to hang on to a teat while the next one is being born, so take careful note of any that seem reluctant to suck. It is a sensible precaution, especially if this is your first litter, to call your vet in to check the bitch and the puppies the day after the birth. It is not strictly necessary, but it lessens the risk of any postnatal infection in the bitch and is a double check that all the puppies are fit and healthy. Any puppies that show signs of abnormality should be put down immediately.

It is virtually impossible to overfeed a nursing bitch, and it is better to feed her three or even four times a day. She will need the best food possible. This should include good raw meat, fish, dampened whole-meal biscuit, eggs, milk and plenty of calcium supplement. The bitch needs the calcium to build strong healthy bone in her puppies, and the drain on her supplies of this can bring on eclampsia.

Whippets are loving and devoted mothers. The same bitch with her three-week-old puppies.

Eclampsia, also known as nursing fever or milk fever, is caused by a shortage of calcium in the bitch. It can occur during pregnancy but is more likely to happen in the second or third week of lactation when the puppies are at their most demanding. The bitch may appear very restless and unsteady on her feet, fall over kicking violently and suffer general body spasms. Call your vet immediately as she will need an injection of calcium into the bloodstream if she is not to die of heart failure. If she has been fed properly during pregnancy and after the birth of the puppies and been given calcium supplements, this is unlikely to happen, but if it does, speed is of the essence if you are to save her.

After three or four days, when the puppies have had their dewclaws removed and you are sure that all is well, the bitch can be moved to where you want to rear the puppies. She needs warmth, peace and quiet during this time, and should not be constantly disturbed by the comings and goings of a busy household. Neither should there be a stream of people looking at the puppies. The most calm and good-tempered bitch can be hyper-sensitive over her first litter and wants only to be left to enjoy them. Time enough for everyone to see them when they are on their feet and running around. It is well to remember, too, that each outsider is a possible source of infection.

If the puppies are being reared outside, the temperature of their quarters must be watched carefully. It is a mistake to keep puppies too warm, but the temperature should ensure that if one rolls away from its mother and the rest of the litter, it will not become chilled. About 68°F (20°C) is required and a large red infra-red bulb, such as those used in piggeries, suspended over the box should enable this temperature to be sustained.

Although the bitch may be a devoted mother, there will be times when she needs to get away from her puppies as they grow larger and more demanding. A small second bed should be placed where the puppies cannot reach her when she feels the need for a little peace and quiet, especially if she is locked in with the litter and cannot get out of the run at will.

The next three weeks are the easy bit. All you have to do is feed your bitch and give her a clean bed whenever necessary. She will do all the work: she will feed the puppies, keep them warm and clean up after them, licking them to make them urinate and defecate. It is instinctive for her to keep her surroundings clean so that there is as little smell as possible to attract predators.

The puppies' claws grow very quickly and from about ten days old, they should be trimmed with a pair of scissors, removing the little white hook on each claw. Otherwise, they can scratch the bitch and make her very sore when they are kneading at her teats to get more milk.

The puppies usually start to open their eyes about twelve to fifteen days after birth, and a week later the first teeth start to appear. By three weeks, they are staggering across the box before falling over on top of their brothers and sisters.

From now on they become the greatest time-wasters ever invented and it is all too easy to spend hours just sitting watching them. In fact it is very important that you do spend time with them for the next few weeks, talking to them and handling them. Their confidence in human beings will be imprinted at this stage in their development, and puppies reared in too great an isolation can become nervous and anti-social later.

Weaning

It is impossible to lay down any hard and fast rule as to when to start weaning the puppies. If the litter consists of only two or three puppies, the bitch may feed them very satisfactorily for a month. However, if it is a large litter of seven or eight, both bitch and puppies may suffer if you do not begin to wean them as early as eighteen days old.

If weaning has to commence very early, you will have to start with milk feeds. Cow's milk is not suitable for puppies as the fat content is not high enough, but there are on the market many powdered brands of milk especially formulated for weaning puppies. These should be made up as directed by the manufacturer. By dipping your finger in the milk and putting it into the puppy's mouth and directing it gently into the bowl you can generally persuade it to lap. You will have to do this with each puppy in turn several times before they have got the idea, and even then they are inclined to get more on, than in, themselves.

Offer them these supplementary feeds four times a day. Twice a day, thicken the milk feed with a baby porridge and sweeten it with a little honey. These feeds should always be given when the bitch has been away from the pups for a while to encourage them to make the effort needed to learn. She is then put back with them, as her milk contains much more goodness than any commercial food, and they need the antibodies she can pass on.

At three weeks plus, the puppies can start on meat. If the litter has not been too large and the dam has been successfully feeding them for this time, it is perfectly reasonable to wean straight on to meat, adding first one, then two, and then three of the milk feeds as each day goes by. How quickly this transition is made depends on the amount of milk the dam is producing, and on the size and number of the puppies.

These first meat meals should consist of scraped beef (shin or skirt are ideal), and a blunt knife makes a good scraping instrument. Each puppy needs a tiny amount only, about the size of a hazel-nut, and must be fed individually to ensure that each gets its fair share. It takes a little time for them to learn how to take it. The enthusiasm for the meat is there; it is the expertise needed to chew and swallow that is lacking. Within a day or so, however, they will all be demanding to be picked up first for their rations, the size of which should be increased slightly day by day.

Now the time-consuming part begins as you gradually take over the responsibility for the puppies from the dam. It cannot be emphasized too clearly that, except in an emergency, this should be a gradual process. The bitch should be allowed as much access to her litter as she wants for the sake of her own health and happiness as much as for the welfare of the pups. The amount of time each bitch spends with her young varies greatly, but this should be her decision and not imposed by you in an effort to speed her return to the show ring, or anywhere else.

During the weaning period, you may find that the bitch is weaning the puppies in her own way by regurgitating some of her food for them. This is a perfectly natural thing for her to do, but if you find that she is doing this, you may have to give her a little extra to make up for what she is passing on to the puppies. It is also wise to cut up her food rather smaller than you would do normally.

By the time the pups are five weeks old, they will need feeding at least four and preferably five times a day. The early morning feed could be milk and cereal with a little tinned puppy meat added, or one of the commercial puppy complete feeds, moistened with milk. At noon, the meal could be scrambled egg, or rusks soaked in milk with a little honey. A bowl of milk and a dry rusk can often be fitted in at tea-time, and then later in the afternoon or early evening, raw minced meat with a good-quality wholemeal puppy-grade biscuit which has been dampened a few hours before with gravy or warm water. Last thing at night, warm milk with cereal or porridge, sweetened with honey, sends them to sleep feeling suitably contented.

Calcium supplement should be added to the evening meal. Com-

At five weeks they enjoy their meals . . .

mercially prepared feeds are vitamized already, and over-supplemen-tation can cause symptoms very similar to those caused by a lack of vitamins or minerals in the diet.

Cooked chicken, rabbit, fish and raw minced tripe are all very suit-able foods for puppies. As a very general rule, meat (or similar high protein food) should form the basis of the meal twice a day, and other meals should consist of more carbohydrate-based ingredients. One of the meat meals should be of fresh red meat and the other of a white meat or fish. At least one of these important (in the eyes of the puppy anyway) meals should be of fresh meat, and the other can gradually be replaced by a commercial food such as tinned puppy food and a mixer biscuit, or one of the puppy complete feeds.

If the puppies have very loose faeces, and you will be doing the clearing up now, feed white meat or fish with rice rather than the raw meat with biscuit. If you step up the carbohydrate intake and cut down

. . . though they are not above a little extra from Mum. It is cruel and unnecessary not to allow a bitch access to her pups for as long as she and they need.

on the protein for a day or so it should clear. If not, call the vet. Puppies can lose condition very quickly if they scour.

Worming

It is as well to assume that despite all your efforts the puppies have been born with worms, as is indeed most likely. If you have wormed the bitch correctly, the infestation will only be light and the puppies will show none of the classic signs of a heavily infested youngster. These are a dull, staring coat and a bloated stomach.

Puppies should only be wormed with the correct type of preparation and you could do great damage by using too strong a medicine. Your vet will be able to provide you with a suitable type and brand of wormer. The fact that most puppies do have worms is another reason

Worming a young puppy. By using a syringe you can ensure that each pup receives the correct dosage.

for keeping children away from very young puppies. When they have been wormed twice, once at three to four weeks and again two weeks later, then they can be introduced to children.

General Hygiene and Welfare

It is very important to keep the puppies' run and kennel immaculately clean, especially in hot weather when there are lots of flies about. Bedding should be changed every day, and runs washed down with disinfectant morning and evening. Do make sure that your disinfectant is suitable for use in kennels. Dogs have very sensitive skins and can react very badly to some substances, but there are many specially prepared disinfectants now on the market. All the faeces should be cleared from the run several times a day as, once again, flies can cause disease.

If the puppies are being reared in the kitchen, you will probably be using newspaper on the floor. This, too, must be constantly changed, not least because tearing it up becomes one of the puppies' favourite games. If the puppies are being reared outside, you can use sawdust on the floor but only if there is sufficient ventilation in the kennel. Otherwise, sawdust can cause eye irritation.

As far as their bedding goes, it is probably best to keep them on the thermal fur bedding on which they were reared. It is easily washed and, until they are completely clean in their kennel, ensures that their coats and skins remain unsoiled. Whippet puppies are very quick to learn cleanliness. It will not be very long before they leave the bed to pass their motions, and by six weeks old they are completely clean in their beds. By the time they are seven or eight weeks old, they will go to the

Puppies need space and amusement. Here, a basket has been turned upside down to provide a safe and interesting playground.

As they get older, they need more space and even more exciting places to explore.

far corner of the run to defecate, and if they have had the freedom to learn good habits, they will be remarkably easy to house-train.

Whether they are reared in the house or in an outside kennel, the puppies should have access to fresh air and freedom to run and play. In good weather they can spend all day outside with a bed somewhere to which they can retire whenever they want to rest. Like small children, puppies need sleep and should not be encouraged to play when they are obviously tired. The size of the run you give them will obviously depend on the size of your garden, but it should be as large as you can manage and escape-proof. It also needs to be safe but with plenty of interest to amuse growing puppies. There should be things to get under and things to climb over, rather like a children's adventure playground.

The puppies should be ready to go to their new homes when they are nine to ten weeks old. It is very wrong to let any puppy go before eight weeks. It is neither physically nor psychologically ready to leave its siblings, its dam or its known and safe environment. At nine weeks plus, they have matured sufficiently to move much more easily, and will settle into their new homes with no trouble at all.

When you receive a telephone call the day after you have sold a puppy telling you how well the puppy has settled in, how happy and outgoing it is, you know that you have done a good job. The care and attention you have given have resulted in a healthy youngster, with a confident and happy temperament, who will give years of devoted companionship and pleasure to his owners.

8

Showing

The Kennel Club

The Kennel Club has as its first aim the general welfare of dogs, but its chief concern is centred on pedigree dogs. It is responsible for the classification of all breeds and the registration of most pedigree dogs in this country. It also sets out the rules and regulations under which shows, field and working trials, and obedience tests are held.

Various other organizations, such as The National Greyhound Racing Club and The International Sheepdog Society, keep breed registers, but for most pedigree dogs and for all those involved in showing, the Kennel Club is the ultimate authority. It is the Kennel Club who grants Challenge Certificates to show societies. A dog has to win three of these certificates, one of them after the age of twelve months and all under different judges, and have had his title confirmed by the authorities, before he may be called a Champion. The judges themselves have to gain Kennel Club approval before they are allowed to award Challenge Certificates and this honour may take many years of experience to achieve.

As the sole authoritative body, the Kennel Club directs the organized activities of pedigree dogs, and can warn off or discipline anyone who participates in any capacity in an unlicensed event. It can also take to task anyone who contravenes the rules at licensed shows, or whose behaviour brings the world of dogs into disrepute. The power and influence of the Kennel Club is far-reaching and, although there are moments when exhibitors might complain about the rules, it is certain that there would be no well-regulated world of dog showing without the Club's control.

Registration

All dogs exhibited at shows subject to Kennel Club Rules have to be registered in the name of the exhibitor. When you buy a pedigree dog, he should have been registered with the Kennel Club and you should have been given his Kennel Club Registration Form. This will give his 'official' name and all the particulars of his parentage, date of birth and breeder. Both you and the present owner sign this form on the back in the section marked 'Application to Register a Transfer', and you then send it to the Kennel Club with the appropriate fee. In due course, you will receive a new Registration Form giving your name as the owner.

If you are buying an older puppy and you wish to show him before the form is likely to be returned (about six weeks) you must add TAF to his name on your entry form for the show. This stands for Transfer Applied For, and indicates that you have both accepted and are willing to abide by the Kennel Club rules.

The Whippet Club Racing Association and The National Whippet Coursing Club also require all dogs to be registered with the Kennel Club. In fact, these bodies are more strict than the Kennel Club itself, as they require a five-generation pedigree for each dog, and this pedigree has to be acceptable to their respective committees before they will issue the passport that will enable a dog to race under WCRA rules. An appointed expert will check the pedigree with the dog standing in front of him, before countersigning the application form, and you would have to be very knowledgeable indeed to falsify a pedigree that would get past these experienced people. If, therefore, you intend not only to show but to race or course your Whippet, make sure that you buy him from a thoroughly reputable breeder. It has been known for a Whippet holding a valid Kennel Club Registration to be refused a racing passport and entry into a coursing club.

If you have bred a litter, it is wise to register the puppies within a few weeks of their birth, and provided both parents are registered there should be no difficulty. The appropriate form, with clear instructions, can be obtained from the Kennel Club. The form has to be signed by the owner of the stud dog as well as by the breeder. All the whelps, their colour and their sex have to be declared on this form, and two names given for each puppy. If you do not initial the appropriate box, and the Kennel Club do not approve of either of the names you have chosen, you may find your puppy with a name selected by the Kennel Club. You may heartily dislike the name but you will be powerless to change it.

Under the present regulations, all puppies must be registered before they are twelve months old. After that age, while theoretically it

The most successful show Whippet in the history of the breed, Ch.
Nutshell of Nevedith. Winner of 36 CCs, 15 Hound Groups and 6
times Best in Show at Championship Shows; and Reserve Best in
Show at Cruft's 1990. Also Top Show Dog, All Breeds, in 1989.

is always possible to register a dog both of whose parents are registered, it could well cost a great deal extra in late registration fees.

Affixes and Prefixes

Established breeders usually have a kennel name registered with the
Kennel Club for their sole use. This is called an affix and is given as
the first name of every dog bred by them. Dogs owned, but not bred
by them, may also carry this kennel name but the affix must be used
as the final part of the name. A registered affix may not be used by
anyone other than the holder for any part of a dog's name. It gives
great pleasure to any breeder to see a dog carrying his affix doing well
in any area of canine activity and also engenders a feeling of permanent responsibility towards all the animals they breed.

Kennel Club Awards

Challenge Certificates   To 'make up' a champion is the dream of every
serious exhibitor. Campaigning a dog to his title is more difficult in

Ch. Nimrodel Wanderer. Record holder for dogs. He has 22 CCs to his credit and is still competing in the ring.

Britain than in most other countries, not least because champions in this country are shown in the Open Classes long after they have become champions. This means that to be awarded a Challenge Certificate the dog must beat all the established winners as well as his peers. Throughout most of the world, the champions compete for Best of Breed only, and a dog can win the equivalent of a CC in the Open Class with no champion opposition.

When you consider that dogs such as Ch. Nimrodel Wanderer, Ch. Welstar Royal Mint and Ch. Selinko Another Lady have in the last few years broken all previous Whippet records and won twenty-two, nineteen and twenty-five Challenge Certificates respectively, it becomes easy to understand the difficulties facing exhibitors. The young bitch Ch. Nutshell of Nevedith, bred by Mr and Mrs J. Barker, owned by Miss Editha Newton and expertly handled by her father, has now surpassed this record and achieved a second by becoming the Top Dog in Britain under the points system operated by the dog journals.

To date, she has won fifteen Groups at Championship Shows and been Best in Show six times as well as achieving Reserve Best in Show at Cruft's. Never before has a Whippet reached such dizzy heights, though some years ago the late Mrs Anne Knight's Champion Dondelayo Duette also went Reserve Best in Show at Cruft's.

Ch. Nimrodel Wanderer was bred by Mrs I. H. Lowe and owned and exhibited by the experienced Mrs June Minns. Ch. Welstar Royal Mint, bred by Mrs Linda Jones was owned and exhibited by Mrs Gwen Hempstock, again an experienced and well-known competitor. Ch. Selinko Another Lady, on the other hand, was bred, owned and exhibited by Mr and Mrs Barry Kennett, who were at that time relative newcomers to the breed, which goes to prove that it is not impossible for a novice, who is quick and willing to learn, to reach the top if they are fortunate enough to have a Whippet who is good enough for high honours.

Ch. Selinko Another Lady. Winner of 25 CCs and Reserve in the Hound Group at Cruft's. She was bred by her owners in their first litter.

Reserve Challenge Certificates   When, at a Championship Show, the judge has in the ring his final line-up of unbeaten dogs, he is looking not just for the ticket winner, but also for a reserve. He has to sign the Reserve Certificate, which carries a statement to the effect that in his opinion this dog 'is of such outstanding merit as to be worthy of being awarded the Challenge Certificate should the Challenge Certificate winner be disqualified'. So although a Reserve CC does not count towards a title, it is still a token of high regard from the judge, and qualifies the recipient for entry in the Kennel Club Stud Book.

The Junior Warrant

This Kennel Club award can be claimed by dogs who have gained twenty-five points between twelve and eighteen months old and therefore out of the Junior Class. There are three points given for a win at Championship Shows at which CCs are on offer, and one point for a win at an Open Show.

Though it is nice to win a Junior Warrant, it is no guarantee of future success. Many a Junior Warrant winner has not realized his early potential, and the converse is equally true in that many a champion did not gain his Junior Warrant. It is certainly not worth ruining a young dog's future chances by over-showing him at an age when he may well be going through an awkward, leggy stage in order to gain this particular award.

Kennel Club Stud Book Number

The Kennel Club keeps a record in its Stud Book of the pedigrees of all winners of a first, second or third prize in the Limit and Open Classes at Championship Shows, and allots such dogs a Stud Book Number, as well as those who gain a Reserve CC. These records are very useful for breeders and essential for historians of a breed.

Licensed Shows

The Kennel Club issues licences for six categories of shows from the informal Exemption Show to the highly organized Championship Show. Most are held in the relatively good weather of summer, but there are shows of one sort of another taking place all over the country throughout the year.

Exemption Shows

Exemption Shows are so called because they are exempt from many of the Kennel Club Rules, though they must have applied for, and been granted, a licence. They may only schedule four or five classes for pedigree dogs but an unlimited number of classes for non-pedigree dogs. Even the pedigree dogs at an Exemption Show need not be registered with the Kennel Club.

These shows are usually held in conjunction with some local event or in aid of a charity. Dogs do not have to be entered in advance, and you merely turn up in good time before the start of judging and the show secretary will take your entry on the field. The classes, which are for both pedigree and non-pedigree dogs, can include 'The Dog in Best Condition' or 'The Dog Most Like Its Owner' (and there have been some startling resemblances seen in that class!). Exemption Shows are intended to be a fun day out for the family and are not to be taken seriously as a measure of your dog's quality, but these shows can be very enjoyable and useful training for a young puppy.

The judges for Exemption Shows can be as varied as the dogs taking part. Sometimes a famous all-rounder, who is normally to be seen judging at Championship Shows, will be there because it is in aid of a favourite charity. Sometimes a local breeder will officiate. It has even been known for celebrities from stage or screen, whose knowledge of dogs is confined to the fact that they have four legs and a tail, to judge at these shows.

Primary and Sanction Shows

All the dogs entered at these shows must be registered at the Kennel Club, but there are considerable restrictions placed on the duration of such shows and the classes they may schedule. There must be only eight classes, with no class higher than Maiden at a Primary Show, and no class higher than Post-Graduate at a Sanction Show. It is virtually impossible for any club to make such shows pay their way, and they are very rarely held these days. This is a pity as they were an excellent training ground for both novice exhibitors and puppies.

Limited Shows

Limited Shows derive their name from the fact that entry is limited to members of the society holding the show. They are usually run by breed clubs, and are the ideal place for both puppies and novice exhibitors to learn their trade. No Challenge Certificate winner can be shown at a Limited Show, but there are very often some excellent youngsters being exhibited. The classification at a Breed Limited Show will be more or less the same as at an Open or Championship Show, as will the number of entries, so there will be a fair selection of dogs.

An invitation to judge a Breed Limited Show is a great honour for an aspiring judge. To have judged at a Breed Show is an important criterion when the Kennel Club come to consider whether a judge is sufficiently experienced to award Challenge Certificates. No amount of Open Show appointments, with four or five classes and a limited number of entries, can compare with the experience gained when facing sixteen to twenty classes with a good entry in each class.

Open Shows

Once again the name of the show is self-explanatory. Open Shows are open to all, and Challenge Certificate winners and even Champions can be entered. Some Open Shows are run by agricultural societies as part of their own annual show; some are run by canine societies and some by breed clubs.

At the first two types of show there will be many breeds represented, each with separate breed classes with their own judge. There might be four classes for each breed, sometimes more, occasionally less. Only rarely will there be sufficient classes to divide the sexes, so dogs and bitches will compete in the same classes. If your breed is not 'classi-fied', i.e. given its own classes, you have to enter in 'Any Variety Not Separately Classified' where it is more likely that you will be judged by an all-rounder than by a breed specialist. At such shows, there is usually a selection of Variety classes, usually judged after Best in Show, in which the dogs of different breeds compete against each other.

Many experienced competitors restrict most of their showing to such Open Shows. They may not like the travelling that is necessary to get to many Championship Shows, which are deliberately scheduled to take place in various areas of Great Britain. The entry fee for Open Shows is much less, and there are enough local Open Shows to pro-vide a day out at most weekends where you can meet friends with a common interest.

Breed Open Shows are in a different category altogether. At these shows, the classification is generous and the judge or judges are nor-mally breed specialists. For them, the opportunity to judge a Breed

Open Show is especially welcomed as such appointments are considered a great honour even by experienced all-rounders who may give CCs in other breeds. For the aspiring breed judge working towards awarding his first set of Challenge Certificates, such an appointment is an important step along the way to giving those precious 'tickets'.

Here you will see many of the up-and-coming young stock in the breed, even some of the Champions. A win at such a show is a win indeed and could bode well for your dog's chances at a Championship Show.

The show calendar is becoming more and more crowded with societies jostling for weekend dates years in advance. In an effort to bring some sensible organization to bear and to make sure that societies in the same area, scheduling the same breeds, do not clash, the Kennel Club has brought in a rule limiting to two the number of Open Shows that a Society may hold on Saturday in any one year. Any other Open Shows they organize will have to be held on Sunday or a weekday.

Championship Shows

Championship Shows are those at which the Kennel Club's coveted Challenge Certificates are on offer. It is only by winning three of these CCs under three different judges that a dog may be titled a Champion – hence the name of this type of show.

Many novice exhibitors are wary about entering a Championship Show, feeling it is all too high-powered for them. It is true that the competition in such a numerically strong breed as Whippets is great and that, as with every other form of competition, it is sensible to gain experience at a less elevated level. Once both you and your dog have done a little winning at Open Shows, however, the time will come when you will want to see how he compares with the best of his breed at a Championship Show. Not until he is in competition with others of top quality will you be able to assess his potential. One can be just as proud of a third prize gained in a good class at a Championship Show as of a first won at an Open Show.

You should not be discouraged if you are not placed the first few times. You are taking on the best of both dogs and handlers. Many of the exhibitors at Championship Shows are seasoned campaigners and know exactly how to present their dogs to the best advantage. They have learnt which judges have a preference for which type of Whippet, and which classes to enter at each stage of the dog's development. There is much to be learnt by just watching such handlers and it is a great mistake, as well as poor manners, to rush away from the show immediately your dog comes out of the ring.

The judge at a Championship Show will be very experienced, whether a breed specialist or an all-rounder. It is a privilege and an honour to be asked to award CCs and the best judges draw large entries. You will sometimes hear criticism of the judging – usually by those who were not placed – but it is well to bear in mind that the judge is merely expressing an opinion. The dogs he placed were the dogs that, in his opinion, corresponded most closely to his interpretation of the Kennel Club Standard for the breed. That interpretation may not be the same as yours, but it is his opinion. You should never show displeasure at your placing and always thank the judge at the end of the day for whatever he may, or may not, have done for your dog.

Ch. Sequence of Shalfleet, winner of 15 CCs and considered by many to be the embodiment of the Breed Standard..

Ch. Oakbark Middleman, a striking red brindle.

Categories of Championship Shows

General Championship Shows   These are organized by large canine
societies, or the canine section of agricultural societies and take place
over two or three days. They feature a wide variety of breeds, which
are divided according to the Kennel Club group system. These are
the Toy, Working, Gundog, Terrier, Utility and Hound Groups, and
all the breeds scheduled within a particular Group will be judged on
the same day.

Most of the numerically strong breeds will have been allocated CCs
for that show, though there are often a few breeds scheduled without CCs. These will be eligible for the Group judging but without CCs
their win cannot qualify them for Cruft's, or count as any award towards a Championship.

The minimum classification for each numerically strong breed will
probably consist of the Cruft's qualifying classes of Minor Puppy,
Puppy, Junior, Post-Graduate, Limit and Open for both sexes. Some
show societies are more generous and will provide Novice, Graduate
or Mid-Limit Classes, and there are some who do not provide a Mi-

nor Puppy Class as they consider that puppies under nine months are too young and immature to be shown. The less popular breeds may have some of the dog and bitch classes combined or miss out the lower classes altogether. Limit and Open Classes are always divided at Championship Shows.

All unbeaten dogs and unbeaten bitches compete for the Dog and the Bitch Challenge Certificates, and the winning dog and bitch then come into the ring for the judge to decide the Best of Breed. It is this Best of Breed who will go forward to represent his breed under the group judge, and the winners of each group will then meet to compete for Best in Show.

Group Championship Shows   These are organized in the same way as the General Championship Shows but cater for only one group. There are two Hound Group Championship Shows in the UK: one is the Houndshow, run by The Hound Association, and the other is the Hound Association of Scotland. Group Championship Shows are of special interest as the classification is generous, and CCs are on offer for all the breeds within the group which have been allocated these by the Kennel Club. Houndshow also schedules such extras as generous prize money, a parade of hunting packs and prestigious Champion Stakes Classes.

Under Kennel Club regulations, both General and Group Championship Shows have to provide suitable benching for all dogs entered at the show. These benches are lines of trestles, divided into compartments on which the dogs can be tethered safely during the show. It is up to each exhibitor to provide whatever bedding he wants for his dog, but a suitable leather collar and a chain are statutory.

Breed Club Championship Shows   It is at these Championship Shows that you will see the very best of the breed. They are run by the breed clubs who provide experienced breed judges and a generous classification. A wide selection of classes of varying levels enables you to select the correct class for the age and maturity of your dog whereas, with the more restricted classes on offer at General Championship Shows, once out of the Junior Class at eighteen months, you may find yourself in the Post-Graduate Class with twenty or more dogs much older and more mature than yours.

Breed Club Shows generally have permission from the Kennel Club to be unbenched, so you have to take a cage or a suitable bed for your dog to rest in during the day.

Cruft's Cruft's is the Kennel Club's own Championship Show, and is the most prestigious show in Britain, probably in the world. It attracts more public and media attention than any of the other Championship Shows held every year, and so in order to keep the number of dogs at a manageable level, it became necessary to impose a qualification in order to enter. A dog has to be a champion, to have his Stud Book number or to have won certain classes during the year at a Championship Show at which CCs were on offer. At the present time, these classes are Minor Puppy, Puppy, Junior, Post-Graduate, Limit and Open, and is the reason that these are the classes scheduled at most general Championship Shows.

For some exhibitors, to qualify to show at Cruft's is a dream fulfilled, and they hardly care whether they are placed or not. It has been said, with some truth, that at Cruft's all the dogs are winners. It is certainly true that Cruft's is like no other show, and most judges would consider it the height of their judging career to be honoured with a Cruft's appointment.

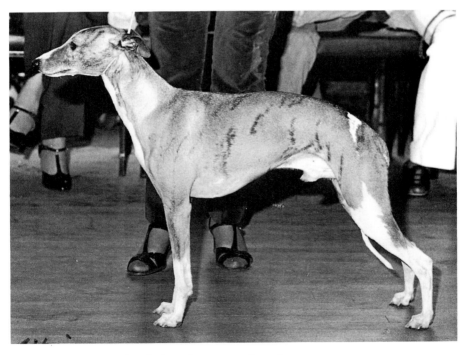

Ch. Novacroft Madrigal, a leading champion in the early 1980s.

*Ch. Dondelayo Duette with her owner and breeder, the late Mrs
Anne Knight. Duette was the first Whippet to achieve Reserve Best
in Show at Cruft's.*

Qualifying for Cruft's can become a mania and it should really be kept in proportion. If your dog is of sufficient quality and you enter him under judges who are likely to appreciate his type, in classes appropriate to his age and maturity, he will certainly qualify at some show, maybe several shows, during the course of the season.

Begin at the Beginning

A great many exhibitors start their showing careers more or less accidentally. They took their dogs to the local village fête and entered the Exemption Show for fun. To their surprise, the dog won, and they were hooked! Showing dogs can become an enjoyable and interesting hobby where you make many new friends. It can be a pleasant day out, away from home responsibilities, a place where you are allowed to indulge in your new hobby without being accused of becoming a bore.

It can also become an obsession, where winning is the only goal and the welfare and happiness of the dog is merely secondary. Of course everyone likes to win, but to be beaten by a good dog is no crime, and the judge is merely expressing an opinion. If you find that winning is all that matters, and you become upset if your dog is not at the head of the line, you should consider a warning, similar to that seen on cigarette advertising, 'Showing dogs can seriously damage your health'.

Training a Show Puppy

If you bought a puppy from a show kennel, it is more than likely that he will already have been trained to stand on a table for a short time, in order that his breeder might assess his make and shape. In this case, all you need to do is to continue doing this every day, rewarding him with a titbit and a pat. Make sure that the table has a non-slip surface – a rubber mat does very well. A minute or two are all that is necessary or he will become bored and begin to resent being made to stand, and once a Whippet had decided that he does not like doing something, he is very difficult to persuade otherwise. He should be placed on the table in the same position as the show Whippets in the photographs, with his hocks at right angles to the ground. If his hind legs are stretched too far behind, he will look cut away over the quarters;

103

*The development of a Whippet puppy. Mrs Webber's Barmoll
Bracken at eleven weeks.*

The same puppy at seventeen weeks.

if they are placed too far under the body, he will look hump-backed. If the puppy is to enjoy showing, he must be comfortable in the position he is being asked to adopt.

The show puppy should be lead trained in the same way as any other, but he should not be made to parade up and down, over and over again. He needs to be taught to come with you happily and if he jumps about a little at first, it is only to be expected.

Five months is quite early enough for ringcraft sessions. Your vet may know where such classes are held and they are a very helpful training ground for both puppy and novice exhibitor. Here you can practise showing the puppy and he can become accustomed to other breeds around him. Whippets are appalling snobs, and prefer to think that they are the only breed, but it is essential that they learn to tolerate the large and the small, the hirsute and the hairless members of their race, even if they do not intend to like them.

Ready for the show ring at six months.

Entering a Show

According to Kennel Club regulations, puppies may be exhibited from the age of six months. However, not all puppies are ready by this stage and it does no harm, and probably a lot of good, to delay your puppy's debut until seven and a half or eight months old. Certainly, unless exactly the right show with exactly the right judge is available, six months is very young to cope with the strain of a long day at a show.

Once you have decided that your puppy is ready, you need to find out about possible shows. There are two weekly dog journals in this country, *Dog World* and *Our Dogs*, in which all shows are advertised, including most local Exemption Shows. You could perhaps begin by entering one of these. However, you are not likely to learn a great deal about serious dog shows at an Exemption Show, and by far the best start for a puppy is a Breed Club Limited or Open Show.

The Kennel Club will give you the name, address and telephone number of your nearest breed club, and if you ring the secretary he will send you a membership form and tell you when their next show is to be held. You will also be sent a schedule for the show, which gives all particulars of the classes and entry qualifications. At Breed Club Shows, you will find everyone very friendly and helpful. The breeder of your puppy will also be prepared to advise you on which classes to enter.

If there is no Breed Club Show scheduled for some months, a local Open Show recommended by the breeder could be a suitable start. Show secretaries are very busy people, and a short letter requesting a schedule and enclosing a stamped, addressed envelope will bring a rapid reply and be more appreciated by them than yet another telephone call at an inconvenient time.

When you have been going to Open Shows for some time, and your dog has had some success, you can enter for a Championship Show. The procedures are much the same, though entries close much further in advance for these shows. You will find many of the same local people and dogs at a Championship Show as at the Open Shows, but there will also be many well-known exhibitors and dogs from much further afield. Take the opportunity to watch the judging, see how the dogs are presented and handled, and try to appreciate why the judge made his selection.

When you receive your schedule, notice the closing date, and fill in the entry form carefully. If your dog's transfer has not yet been returned by the Kennel Club, you must add TAF (Transfer Applied For) to his name. If even his original registration has not arrived, you may still enter but must add NAF (Name Applied For) as well. Make sure that you post off the entry in good time. It is a very sensible precaution, especially if it is near to the closing date, to get a Proof of Posting slip from the Post Office. This costs nothing and can save a lot of dispute later if your entries get lost or delayed in the post.

Preparation for the Show

Whippets are comparatively easy to prepare for the ring. They need virtually no trimming though a little judicious tidying up can be done. Some exhibitors remove the whiskers, in the odd belief that it gives the dog a neater appearance. Whiskers are a dog's radar and it is most unkind and unnecessary to cut them off. Nails should be trimmed at least a few days before the show, and teeth cleaned.

If you have a Whippet with a lot of white, it may be necessary to bath him the day before the show, otherwise the usual good grooming is all that is needed. Kennel Club regulations forbid the use of chalk if it is left in the coat, but chalk or baby powder can be used to clean up a white coat if it is completely brushed out before going to the show. If your dog has a dark coat, such as a brindle, blue or black, it is fatal to bath him for at least a week before a show. Those dark-skinned dogs nearly all develop a fine scurf after bathing which gets worse the more you brush.

Whippets are running hounds and should not be shown fat and lacking in muscle-tone. This does not mean that the dog must be in top racing or coursing condition, merely that he must look sleek and elegant. It is a beauty competition – not an athletics meeting – but most dogs, like people, look and move better when they are fit and not carrying extra weight.

The Evening Before

It is advisable to get all the things you will need ready the evening before as most shows necessitate an early start. Your show bag should contain:

A clean, thick, comfortable rug for the dog to lie on whether the show is benched or not.

A suitable collar and benching chain as stipulated under Kennel Club rules. It is all too easy for a bored Whippet to chew through a leather lead, and it is all too easy to imagine the resulting disaster.

A show lead.

A rubber grooming brush and silk or velvet square.

A damp flannel in a plastic bag and a small dry towel for cleaning muddy feet.

A small spray bottle of a suitable disinfectant for wiping the dog down on return to the car. This is especially useful if you have other dogs – not all exhibitors are as meticulous as they should be over their dogs' health and you will not want to carry any infection home.

A small bowl for water, milk or whatever food you wish to give the dog at the show.

A coat for the dog to wear on the bench if necessary. Whippets are not likely to show their best if they have been hunched up shivering all morning.

Your own picnic lunch and refreshments in a Whippet-proof container.

The schedule of the show as a reminder of what classes you entered, together with any passes for the show sent to you in advance, and a show clip for your ring number.

Show Day

Every dog should have time to relieve himself properly before travelling long distances to a show. It is unwise to feed a puppy before a car journey and in this way both he and you will arrive in a much better state.

Leave yourself plenty of time to get to the showground. Your puppy will be much happier and show much better if he has had time for a run in the car park on arrival. On entering the showground, your first consideration should be for the dog, so settle him comfortably before greeting friends. Most Whippets prefer benched shows where they can be warm, snuggled into their own rugs and out of the way of trampling feet, though it may take a puppy some time to become used to being chained and left, and you should not leave him unattended until you are sure he is settled.

Unbenched shows are another occasion at which collapsible wire cages are invaluable, providing the dog with his own area in which he can rest in safety. It is well worth the effort involved in carrying them into the showground, even though it may mean two journeys from the car park. It also means that you have more freedom of movement to look at the stalls and chat to friends without dragging a tired and reluctant puppy along with you.

While in the ring, every exhibitor has to wear a card bearing a number. The numbers of all those entered in the class are given in the catalogue for the show, together with all particulars of the exhibitor and the dog. The numbers only are in the judge's book so, in theory, he does not know the names of the dogs in front of him.

There are various ways in which these ring cards are distributed. Cruft's, for example, send the ring numbers out to every exhibitor before the show, and the ring number also acts as your entry card to the showground; but at most Championship Shows, the ring numbers are put on the exhibitor's bench and it is all too easy to find that your ring number is under the dog you have just settled down so comfortably. For these large shows, separate entry passes are sent out by the printers to every exhibitor well in advance, but if your passes have not arrived several days before the show, it is advisable to telephone the secretary. It is always stated clearly in the schedule if passes are *not* being sent out.

For most Open Shows, passes are not sent out and ring numbers are distributed by the steward in the ring. Breed Shows do not send out passes either and they often have their ring numbers ready for collection at the door. It is as well to make sure on arrival which method of distribution is in operation so that you have no last minute panic.

At the end of the day, remember that your dog will be as exhausted as you are. He may appear to have slept all day, but the mental stress of showing is great and you will find he is very tired next day. Whether he won or lost, whether he behaved as if he had had no training at all or showed like a little angel, he is still the same dog you took to the show. He loves you as much as ever and wherever he came in his class, you should feel the same way about him.

9

Judging

If you exhibit regularly and with moderate success, sooner or later you will be asked if you would like to judge. It does not require a high degree of academic achievement to become a competent judge, but it does need a professional approach to the task. People pay to exhibit their dogs, and they have a right to expect a fair assessment based on a reasonable degree of knowledge and experience on the part of the judge.

Before accepting a judging appointment, you need to be confident that you can make a reasoned appraisal of a Whippet, so studying both the Kennel Club Standard of the breed, and the Illustrated Standard issued by the Whippet Breed Council is essential in building up the necessary knowledge. You should also have a clear mental picture of the type of Whippet you like, and feel able to justify your preferences with reference to these Standards.

An excellent way to learn about the nuts and bolts of ring management, is to offer to steward. Most experienced judges and stewards are very happy to help those anxious to learn, and it can be very instructive to watch these judges handle each dog in exactly the same way and give each one the same amount of attention.

An expert steward is of the greatest assistance to a judge, placing the dogs already seen into correct order and informing him of which classes they have come from. Such a steward will have the judge's book ready in order that the judge may take any notes on his winners, and all the prize cards and rosettes organized and ready to hand out. All this should be done in an unobtrusive manner – it is the judge, not the steward who is in charge of the ring. As an aspiring judge, however, there is much to learn from a really experienced steward about the best way in which to organize a ring, and it is very helpful to have the opportunity to see the whole procedure from the inside.

As a seasoned exhibitor, you will be aware of the criticisms levelled at judges. It is impossible for a judge to please everyone and, indeed, he is not there to please anyone but himself. The job of the judge is to offer his opinion on the relative merits and qualities of the Whippets exhibited on the day, and to do this without fear or favour.

An extra layer of skin is a prerequisite for judging, as there will be times when the dog belonging to a good friend must be left out and that of an old rival placed at the head of the line-up. In fact, if you are concentrating entirely on the dogs as you should be, and not looking up the lead, it is not until the end of the class that you become aware of the owners of those dogs you have placed. Judges have to be prepared to take the brickbats as well as the bouquets, to do the job honestly and to the best of their ability, even when their decisions may not be popular with their friends.

If you do this, you will be asked to judge a second time and then again, until the privilege of being asked to judge first a Breed Club Show, and finally to award Challenge Certificates becomes a possibility.

The First Appointment

One of the nicest jobs for the secretary of a canine society is to telephone a prospective judge with an invitation, but this alone does not constitute a contract and the invitation must be confirmed and accepted in writing by both parties. Once accepted formally, a contract is deemed to have been made. If a judge does not fulfill an appointment, the Kennel Club is informed and will only be satisfied with the most genuine of reasons. Last minute stage fright is not acceptable!

Before the day of the show, the secretary will send a schedule with the entry numbers marked, and will let you know what time you may expect to be in the ring. Until then, you will probably have nightmares in which you are presiding over a totally empty ring, but in fact first-time judges usually draw a good entry. After all, no one knows which dog you may put up, and who can resist giving it a try?

Show Day

You will need to take a reliable pen and a pad for your notes on the winning dogs or, if you possess one, a small tape-recorder. If you have not used a tape-recorder before, it is as well to practise with it at home, so that you are thoroughly familiar with the mechanism.

The amount of time spent on deciding what to wear will depend on your sex. There is not a lot of choice for the men, but do remember to take the vagaries of the British weather into account.

For women, however, dress can be more important. It is essential to be comfortable: the weather can be unpredictable and Whippets are not very big dogs, which means a lot of bending and stooping. Trousers can look smart, but then one usually wears trousers as an exhibitor, so it is a pleasant change to wear different apparel as a judge and go looking the part. A suit with a pleated skirt is safe and easily adapted to suit the weather. If the show is outside, sensible shoes are a must, unless you want to spend the day pulling your high heels out of the ground. Even with an indoor venue, too high a heel can be dangerous in that you may step backwards onto a dog's paw.

A spare pair of tights, and a second pair of shoes could well make the difference between a good day and a thoroughly uncomfortable one. You should also avoid wearing jewellery, which might dangle over the dog while you are examining him, and which might prove too great a temptation for a puppy.

If, by some miracle, it is a very hot day and you are judging outside, a suitable hat will prevent you getting too red and flustered, but one with a small neat brim, not a large straw hat which might frighten the dogs. Bare arms should also be avoided in hot weather as standing in a grass ring for a couple of hours without a break can lead to a nasty case of sunburn.

Make sure to arrive at the show in very good time. The first thing to do is to report to the secretary, who will not only provide you with a coffee but give you your judging book. You can save time in the ring by signing the pages of your book before you start so that only the winners' numbers have to be entered.

Ring Manners

There are some judges under whom it is always a pleasure to show. Their impeccable behaviour towards all their exhibitors makes each one feel that he is being given every consideration. Even when such a judge has not placed a particular dog, he will have handled him gently and looked at him carefully before forming his opinion. There is absolutely no excuse for a judge to handle the dogs roughly or to show by his manner what his opinion of any exhibit might be.

Kennel Club regulations state that there shall be no conversation in the ring with the judge, and this rule should be strictly adhered to by both judge and exhibitor. No matter how well you know the exhibitor, it is unwise and gives other competitors a bad impression if you call them by name – it is much better to stick to the old-fashioned

Ch. Tilegreen Tornado. He shared top honours in 1989 with the record-holding Ch. Nimrodel Wanderer.

Sir or Madam. A polite please and thank you is also appreciated, as is a friendly smile and a pat for the dog.

Experienced exhibitors will understand and appreciate a little more time being spent on the puppies, or on a novice exhibitor, but apart from this, all exhibits are worthy of equal consideration. If, at the end of the day, those whose dogs were not placed are still smiling, you have managed to achieve the right balance, and have probably done a good job.

Ring Management

When all the dogs in the class have entered the ring and been stood, it is a good beginning to have them all move round the ring twice. This gives the dogs, especially the puppies, time to settle and gives you a good view of their profile movement, which is always very important. Do not try to follow each dog as he moves round, but choose a point from which you can watch them following each other in a straight line across your view.

Give each exhibitor time to set his dog up on the table before standing back and taking a look at the overall picture before you. If you

Ch. Welstar Royal Mint. This may not be the usual show pose for a champion, but it does illustrate the lovely forward stride that earned him 19 CCs.

have been watching experienced judges, you will have seen that though each may have his own way of examining the dogs individually, he does not vary that method from dog to dog. Most judges start their examination, logically enough, with the head and proceed from there, but the exact order is not important. What is important is that you examine each dog in the same way.

There is a very good reason for asking exhibitors to walk their dogs in a triangle, and that is the question of time. If the ring is of a fair size and the dogs can be moved in a triangle, you will have the opportunity to view hind, profile and front movement in a much shorter space of time than if they have to move up and down the ring twice. Of course, at many indoor shows, there may not be the space in which to move the dogs in a triangle, in which case you will have to ask each exhibitor to move up and down the ring twice. The first time, you will be able to assess the hind and front movement, and then you will have to move to the side to view the profile movement. Hopefully you will not have too many exhibitors who insist on walking between you and the dog!

When you have looked at all the dogs, you can ask the exhibitors to stand their dogs for you to make your decisions. Here it will be the overall balance and quality of the dog that will take your eye. You may have discovered, upon individual examination, the faults of each one and it should be remembered that the perfect specimen has yet to be whelped. How serious you consider these faults to be will depend, to a certain extent, on your interpretation of the Standard. However, balance, movement and that indefinable thing called quality can offset minor faults, and should have considerable influence in making your final choice.

If there are a lot of dogs in a class, you may need to whittle down the numbers before making a final choice. In this case, you should make it clear that you are not pulling the dogs out in any particular order. It would be very tactless to pull out only six dogs as this will mean that when your line-up is complete, only one dog will leave the ring without a card. If you cannot make your final decisions

Ch. Martinsell Wild and Lonely. The only blue champion there has been in the UK.

immediately, it is more considerate to your exhibitors to pull seven or eight dogs in before making your eventual choice of the final five. It is Kennel Club regulations that the winning dogs are lined up from left to right in front of the judge.

The numbers of the winning dogs are then entered in the judging book, the prize cards are handed out by the ring steward and you make notes on the winners in each class for your judge's report.

Judge's Critique

Exhibitors can be very disappointed if the judge does not write a report on the winning dogs and send it to both the weekly dog papers. The papers usually request such a report and supply an envelope, but even if they do not, it will be looked for eagerly by those who paid you the compliment of entering their dogs in order to have your opinion. It is only good manners, therefore, to write a critique and if you find this tiresome you should consider yourself lucky that you have not been judging in Europe where the judge has to write a critique on every dog entered.

Ch. Samoems Silent Knight of Shalfleet. Bred by Tim Teillers in Holland from Shalfleet lines, this was the first imported Whippet to become a UK champion.

When you read some judges' reports on their winning dogs, you might wonder why they awarded them a prize at all. They seem to consider it necessary to find fault with every dog reviewed. There must have been good reasons why the dog was placed first, and it is these good points that should be commented on, not his faults pointed out for future reference. It is much better to say, for instance, that you preferred the movement of your winner than it is to say that the dog who came second did so because he moved badly behind.

When you get home, you may well feel that you made a mistake in some class or other, and that you should have put dog A over dog B. No judge, if he is honest with himself, feels he has got it right every time. Under pressure, with the steward looking at the clock and several more classes to get through, errors of judgement are easy to make. With experience you learn to accept this and to make a mental note not to commit that particular error next time. Given time, you might even learn to enjoy judging!

10

The Coursing Whippet

The hounds that hunt by sight rather than by scent are called sight-hounds or gazehounds, and this method of hunting by sight is known as coursing. It is the way many predators hunt their quarry and for hundreds of years coursing hounds have been used to kill hares. In fact, in the Middle Ages, only the local Lord of the Manor was allowed to own a Greyhound. This was to ensure that a mere peasant might

A good hand massage helps prepare the muscles for the task ahead.
Miss Susan Baird with Tweseldown Woodlark.

not be tempted to poach his Lordship's game in order to feed his hungry family. There is still a great deal of informal, unorganized coursing with cross-breds and lurchers today in which the object of the exercise is less to test their dogs than to catch a hare for the pot.

Coursing under National Coursing Club rules has been defined as 'a competitive test of the merits of coursing dogs – two dogs only in each course – under formalized conditions regulated by a strict and detailed code of rules'. The object is not to catch and kill the hare, but to test the speed, agility, determination and courage of the dogs. The rules of the National Whippet Coursing Club are basically the same as those of the National Coursing Club for Greyhounds, with minor alterations to take into account the difference in size.

Meetings take place from about the middle of September, when the harvest is finished, until the beginning of March. Although there is no official 'close' season for hares, it is forbidden by the Hares Preservation Act of 1892 to sell hares between March and July, and no sportsman would wish to jeopardize the future of this marvellous species. Hares are not, however, the working farmers' favourite form of wildlife as three hares can consume as much feed as one sheep, and it is mainly on sporting estates where coursing takes place that they are allowed to flourish. Only a very small hare population would be tolerated by the more commercial farms.

The Coursing Clubs

In the past, Greyhounds could only be owned by those with land and position, and it was not long before tales of a particular dog's prowess in the field resulted in competitions between neighbours' dogs. From these private duels grew the desire to test the dogs in public competition and the formation of coursing clubs. The first of these clubs was the Swaffham Coursing Club, which was established in 1776 and is still running meetings today. By 1858, there were so many coursing clubs that the National Coursing Club was formed to regulate and control coursing. Today, there are still twenty Greyhound coursing clubs running meetings throughout the season. Greyhounds compete not only for the sport, however; the prize money or 'purse' can be very generous and there is much betting on the outcome.

Whippet coursing, like Whippet racing, is strictly amateur; no prize money or betting is allowed and the owners run their dogs purely as a test of their working ability.

The first club to be formed to run Whippets was The Whippet Coursing Club, established in 1962 by five people Miss Carpenter, Mrs McKay (Laguna), Mr Riviere, Mr Scrimegour and Mrs Ticehurst (Porthurst). So, right from the start, coursing had the support of well-known show breeders. It follows that among those they approached for support were fellow exhibitors and breeders of show stock. Many famous prefixes appeared on the running cards: Ballagan, Dragonhill, Martinsell, Padneyhill, Shalfleet, and Tweseldown amongst them. Many dogs running today still carry these prefixes or have them in their pedigrees.

The East of England Whippet Coursing Club was formed in 1970 by the Hon. Mrs Richardson (Hungry Hall) and its meetings are held mainly in Essex and Cambridgeshire. A year later, Mrs Gilpin (Wenonah) and Mrs Webb (Padneyhill) started the East Anglian Whippet Coursing Club and, in 1973, Mr Jarvis established the Woolley Whippet Coursing Club whose meetings are held around Huntingdon.

These are the only four Whippet coursing clubs running under rules in the country. They have a central body, The National Whippet Coursing Club (whose present secretary is Miss Baird), which is represented on the British Field Sports Coursing Committee.

All four clubs have a waiting list for membership, and it may take several years before graduating from being a non-running member to becoming a full running member of a club. During the time you are a non-running member, you will be expected to attend some meetings every year to help walk the fields and learn about the sport.

A Coursing Meeting

A running member of a club is sent an entry form for each meeting. This gives the stakes to be run, which will be divided in various ways. There may be a stake for dogs and a stake for bitches, or they may be divided by height or weight. Most stakes consist of eight runners and are run on a knock-out system, the winning dog of each pair going forward to the next round. The finalist, therefore, will have to run three times and will need both courage and stamina to win the last round. Only occasionally will one owner get two runners, as there are always more dogs entered than places in the stakes.

Most Whippet coursing meetings are 'walked', which means that those taking part walk across the fields in a straight line, stopping when

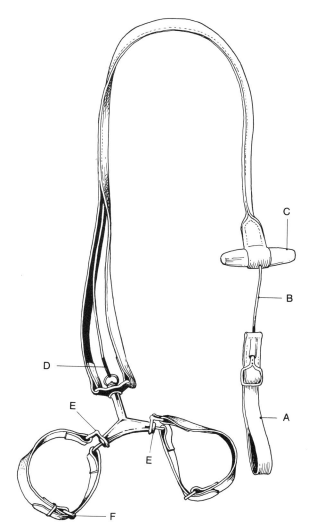

A pair of coursing slips.

One end of each collar is attached to a metal bar (F). The other end has a strong spigot which slots into the metal with a spring attachment (E). A cord is attached to the spring (D) and runs up the lead ending in a wrist strap (A). This cord is longer than the leather lead (B) which finishes with a wooden toggle (C). The slipper puts the strap round his wrist and holds the lead by the toggle. When he has the dogs sighted and the hare at the required distance, he releases the toggle, and the strength of the dogs, who are straining to go, pulls back the spring contained within the metal bar, opening both collars. (See also photograph on page 122)

121

The dogs are put into slips with the red collar on the left and the
white collar on the right. The dogs' heads are held side by side until
the slips are released so that neither should have an advantage.

a hare gets up. The two dogs competing against each other are put
into 'slips', that is a special set of double collars on a single leash that
has a quick release mechanism. The slipper walks out in front of the
field. Slipping is a great art, and slippers at official meetings hold a
licence from The National Coursing Club, which is far from easy to
obtain. The object is to make sure that both dogs have seen the hare
and neither has an initial advantage over the other.

The dog on the right-hand side wears a white knitted collar and
the dog on the left-hand side a red one. This enables the judge, who
is on horseback, to differentiate between them, and when he has finished judging the course, he will pull out a corresponding red or white
handkerchief to indicate the winning colour. The judge, too, has many
years of experience and holds a NCC licence. He will ride to one side
of the field in order to be in a position to keep the dogs in view but
not to interfere in any way with the natural running of the hare.

When the hare has been given a lead of the distance stipulated in the rules, that is not less than 35 yards (32 metres), the slipper releases the dogs and they set off after the hare. The judge follows and awards each dog points for the manner in which he runs and causes the hare to twist and turn. Points are awarded for speed, making the hare turn or jink, and for going past the other dog.

Hares can and do turn much faster than any hound, and the lead that it is given ensures that most hares will escape. Only an exceptionally good Whippet can catch and kill a young fit hare, and even then the hare would have to behave in an uncharacteristically foolish manner. That being said, not all adults are young and fit, so it follows that some are killed. It is against the National Coursing Club rules to course leverets, or hares that show signs of having been coursed previously.

The art of slipping the dogs so that they get away together with no advantage to either, and that of judging the points scored during the course by each dog, are highly skilled tasks; and it takes much practice and experience before a licence to judge or slip at official coursing meetings will be granted by the National Coursing Club.

A few Whippet coursing meetings are 'driven'. This means that the hares are driven by a line of beaters towards the slipper holding the two competing dogs. The field will be instructed as to where they are

When the hare has been given the correct lead, the slipper releases the dogs. Here Laguna Black Larmite (white collar) establishes an early lead.

123

This is what happens to the less agile! Red collar has completely missed the turn.

to stand so as not to obstruct the course or prevent the hare from using his natural escape routes.

All hares at all meetings are wild and have not been displaced from their familiar surroundings. The notion that hares are shipped to unfamiliar grounds and released for the dogs probably originated from the old miners' rabbit coursing meetings.

Coursing is the ultimate test of a Whippet, and it is a most thrilling experience on a fine autumn morning to watch your dog galloping over the fields, jumping ditches or walls or battling his way through

Great stamina, courage and agility are required as hares are very fast, can turn on their tracks in an instant and, running on their own home territory, know every inch of the ground. Tweseldown Lengoldstick (white collar) and Laguna Black Larmite (red collar) do battle.

It's all in a day's sport. The performance of each dog comes under close scrutiny.

a hedge. It has to be said, though, that such idyllic days are offset by those that consist of a cold, wet struggle over heavy plough with the rain gradually soaking down inside your shirt and your boots. It says much for the determination of both owners and dogs that some very good coursing can be seen on such days.

In his book *Lurchers and Longdogs*, Colonel Walsh quotes the Greek, Arrian, writing eighteen hundred years ago as saying: 'The true sportsman does not take out his dogs to destroy the hares, but for the sake of the course, and the contest between the dogs and the hares, and is glad if the hare escapes.' This famous quotation certainly reflects the view of coursing held by those who take part in the sport, but if one is against such activities there is no obligation to take part.

Dual-Purpose Breeding

From the beginning of formal Whippet coursing there have been experienced breeders prepared to test their show stock under sporting conditions. Such breeders believe that only in this way can the continued freedom of the Whippet from genetic malformations be guaranteed. It takes considerable courage to risk a show dog on the field, particularly a youngster just beginning to hit top form in the ring. However, it is a tremendous thrill to see a beautiful specimen of this elegant breed, who only two days ago was gliding around a show ring, streaking across a field in front of his opposition. It is this ability still to fulfil his proper function that makes a Whippet such a special dog.

Of course, it is not necessary to work your dogs in order to produce healthy stock, though all Whippets need a certain amount of free running. It has often been said that fanciers only hold their breed in trust for the future, and working your stock is one way of ensuring that those faults that might cause problems to a running dog are not encouraged. When the committee of The Whippet Club drew up the first Standard for the breed, they had the function for which the breed was intended in mind. All the exaggerations that have crept in to make the show Whippet more elegant and eye-catching have been at the expense of this functional ability. If such selective breeding continues too long, Whippets, like Greyhounds, will divide into two breeds.

The show Greyhound is bred solely for its looks and is judged entirely by the standards of the beauty contest whereas the coursing

Ch. Sound Barrier. The first bench champion to win a major Open coursing stake. He was also a top coursing stud dog.

Ch. Chyton Copy-Press. The only other bench champion to win an Open coursing stake. Copy-Press is out of Sound Barrier's litter sister by a son of Ch. Deepridge Mintmaster.

Greyhound is judged solely by performance. How good looking he may or may not be is totally irrelevant. Hence the development of two entirely separate types to the detriment of both.

The division into working or show Whippet has not overtaken this breed, and there are many examples of dual-purpose animals today. From the beginning of Whippet coursing under rules, top show dogs have competed in the field, and sporting kennels have used carefully selected show champions in their breeding programmes. As long as this continues, Whippets will remain free from many of the distressing genetic faults of other breeds.

A true dual-purpose sporting Whippet, WCRCh. Madishan Moonlake. One of the few pedigree Whippets who could beat the cross-breds on the track. He also won the Whippet Coursing Club's Nicholl Cup three times in succession and it was then replaced by the trophy called the Moonlake Cup in his honour.

The Working Whippet

If you intend to course your Whippet, or to work him with rabbits either lamping or ferreting, it is a wise precaution to buy the puppy from a sporting kennel. This will give you the best chance of obtaining a dog with the steady temperament needed, as well as the speed and substance for work. A puppy bred purely for racing may be very fast indeed, and love to chase, but may lack the bone and substance for a long day in the field. Racing Whippets are handicapped on weight, so that there has been much selective breeding for lighter bone, less body weight and more length of leg. The substantial rib cage, giving great heart and lung capacity, which is called for in the Standard, is less necessary when sprinting the distances favoured by the racing clubs. A working Whippet, however, needs great stamina if he is to spend long hours, not always in the best of weather, out in the fields.

The matter of height also needs to be considered. The coursing clubs enforce a strict height maximum of 20 inches (51 centimetres), and kennels breeding dual-purpose or sporting Whippets are very careful to bear this in mind within their breeding programmes. If your ambition is to course under rules, selecting a puppy from correct-size stock will enhance your chances of obtaining a dog of the desired size.

Rearing a Working Puppy

There should be no difference in the way a pet, show or working puppy is reared. All puppies need good food, gentle exercise, warmth and love. The only way in which training might vary is that a Whippet intended to race or work can be encouraged to chase from an early age by playing games in which a lure is dragged in front of him. Even this game, beloved by all Whippet puppies, should not be overdone or the puppy will get bored.

It is also a sensible idea, if coursing is what you have in mind, to accustom the puppy to walking by the side of another dog, on a short double lead, away from you. Such training, however, is best left until he is at least nine months old, and the other dog must be absolutely reliable.

Whippets will chase quite naturally, and the main difficulty any Whippet owner has is teaching him to differentiate between what constitutes legal quarry and that which is strictly forbidden.

11

The Racing Whippet

Whippet racing was a popular sport in the north of England long before the breed was recognized by the Kennel Club, and before such a creature as a 'pedigree' Whippet was known. These early racing Whippets could weigh as little as seven pounds (3 kilograms) and were raced together with small lurchers and terriers.

Racing was to the 'rag', which is to say that the dogs raced up a straight track towards their owners who would be shouting and waving a rag which the dog would grab at the end of the race. Starting traps were unheard of, and the dogs were started by a 'slipper', a man who held them by the collar and the base of the tail and threw them off their marks. It was a great art to project the dog as far forward as

Racing is a good family day out.

possible and have him land on his feet and in his stride. The starting judge would impose severe penalties for slipping dogs too early, and there were also penalties for slipping them too slowly, a trick sometimes used to beat the bookmakers!

The earliest book on Whippet racing was written in 1894 by Freeman Lloyd of the National Whippet Racing Club, and the sport was taken very seriously by the owners. A good dog that was capable of winning races could add considerably to the income of the family in hard times, and was given the treatment and care that would keep him in top form. Pedigree was of no importance – speed was the only criterion – and a little terrier or Greyhound blood might be bred into a line to improve speed or provide a little sharpness.

All this is a far cry from modern Whippet racing, with its electrically controlled traps and mechanical lures, but enthusiasm for the sport shown by both the dogs and their owners has not changed. Just as much thought and attention goes into the training and feeding of their charges nowadays, though it is doubtful if anyone has to go short to provide the Whippet with his supper. Whippet racing today is very much a family sport, with wives, husbands and children enjoying the day out, having a picnic during the comparative peace while the dogs are weighed-in, and discussing the relative chances of the dogs in each race. Once racing has started, the noise level rises considerably, with much vocal encouragement from the family of each dog as they fly up the final straight, compounded by the barking of other canine contestants eager for their turn.

Non-Pedigree Whippet Racing

A major advance in the development of Whippet racing came in 1967 when the British Whippet Racing Association was formed. The Association's aims are 'to promote greater friendship and understanding between the Whippet racing clubs; to give strength to the advancement of the sport; to help clubs in dealings with local councils in negotiation for land, and to control and standardize Whippet racing'.

The BWRA is made up of ten regions, each of which is run by its own committee according to the rules of the Association. They have periodic national committee meetings, with representatives from all ten regions, which are presided over by the executive committee. A member of any club that is affiliated to the BWRA can join the Association through the club secretary and is then entitled to participate in Association events. All dogs must be registered and registration cards are issued which have to be produced at Association events. The BWRA does not require that a dog is a pure-bred Whippet, though he must be of 'Whippet type', and many of their top dogs have Greyhound blood three or four generations back.

For the National Championships, the dogs are run in two-pound (1-kilogram) weight divisions from 16 to 32 pounds (7 to 14.5 kilograms). To run in the Championships, a dog must have come first or second in a qualifying heat at his home club, and competition is very stiff. If he wins his final, the dog attains the prefix 'Racing Champion', but this title will not be recognized by the Kennel Club, and could not be used in any context other than racing.

The BWRA does not award prize money at its national race meetings, though the regions are allowed to do so. It was this lack of monetary reward which saw the formation in 1976 of the National Whippet Racing Federation. Federation meetings are held at affiliated club venues over different running distances, with good prize money and trophies.

The Whippet Club Racing Association

It was the formation of the BWRA that led to the setting up of the Whippet Club Racing Association a year later. The Whippet Club, which is the oldest of the breed clubs, felt it was responsible for ensuring that Whippets did not split into two different breeds, as had happened with Greyhounds, with show dogs being registered with the Kennel Club, and racing stock with the BWRA. It, too, wished to promote, organize and standardize Whippet racing, but under the control of a responsible breed club and within the auspices of the Kennel Club.

The WCRA is an association of racing clubs, each of which has agreed to abide by the rules of the Association. Racing procedure is laid down by the committee of the WCRA but any change in the rules has to be referred to the parent club, The Whippet Club.

Dogs are issued with a racing passport, made out in the Kennel Club registered name of the Whippet and giving the name under which he will race, his Kennel Club number, his WCRA number and all other relevant facts. The passport also has a photograph and gives detailed markings of the animal. Before a WCRA passport is issued, the owner has to produce the Kennel Club registration and a five-generation pedigree of the dog and to fill in an application form signed by the breeder. All the papers will be countersigned by one of the officials appointed by the WCRA, who will wish to see the dog and not just the pieces of paper. It has been known for a dog, with a valid Kennel Club registration, to be refused a passport because there was reasonable doubt about the true pedigree background of the animal. This is one of the reasons why you should buy a puppy from a reputable breeder if you might want to race your Whippet with the WCRA.

The Kennel Club has granted the WCRA the right to award dogs who win two finals in their weight group at Championship meetings the title of 'Whippet Club Racing Champion'. This is usually shortened to WCRCh. and can be used on pedigrees made out by breeders, although the Kennel Club would not use the title on official pedigrees issued by them.

There are usually four Championship meetings each season, two of which will be run over 150 yards (137 metres) on a straight track, and two over 240 yards (219 metres) round a track with two bends. The WCRA also divides dogs into two-pound (1-kilogram) classes from 'not exceeding 16lbs' (7kg) to 'not exceeding 30lbs' (13.5kg). The races are run off scratch with each weight group divided into heats, with the first two from each heat going forward to the next round. This sometimes means, if there is a large entry, that the dogs have to run four times in an afternoon.

The various clubs affiliated to the WCRA hold 'Open' meetings where the best dogs from other clubs as well as the home club, compete for trophies and points in the Superstars League. Competition is keen, with many WCR champions and potential champions taking part, as well as good club dogs. Those knocked out in the first round usually have their own consolation trophies, so that all the dogs get more than one chance to win something. The clubs vary both the length of the races and the system of handicapping from meeting to meeting. There are meetings at which the dogs are graded according to past performance in order that as many dogs as possible have the chance to win a race, as well as the usual weight handicap meetings. If their grounds allow, the clubs also run different lengths of race from the 150-yard straight to 240-yard bend meetings. Some clubs even run longer distances, so that the dogs who may lack sprint speed but have strength and stamina, may have their chance.

They're off! The handicapping system can be clearly seen.

Approaching the lure. The Whippet's braking system is effective but puts great strain on legs and feet.

Owners pick their dogs up. Some are easier to remove from the lure than others!

Buying a Whippet for Racing

If you wish to buy a potential racing champion, the most sensible course of action is to go to a good racing kennel. Whippets bred for racing have been bred with speed as the chief criterion, which is not to say that they do not have the usual lovely Whippet temperament but, with few exceptions, they would be unlikely to win any prizes in the top beauty competitions of the Championship Show ring. Because the handicapping system is based on weight, there is a tendency for racing bred dogs to have less bone and substance for their height than show or coursing stock. This is one of the reasons why, although there have been bench champions who have won Open coursing stakes, there have been no dual show/racing champions.

There are dual-purpose kennels who have had a considerable influence on racing stock, notably Chancerick, Laguna, Martinsell, Russettwood and Summersway, and knowledgeable racing breeders continue to go back to successful show sires from time to time to improve conformation. However, it is with a racing-bred puppy that

WCRCh. Jolly (Casaloma Sea Pigeon). The supple back needed for great sprint speed is clearly shown here.

WCRCh. Pebbles (Pippawood). The other extreme extension of a racing Whippet. The length of stride of the top racers is seen in this picture.

you are most likely to have success on the track. The extra turn of speed needed to win in top-class competition is more likely to be found in a Whippet bred by an expert in this field than in a puppy bred by someone whose main interests lie elsewhere.

If, however, you are less competitive and only wish to race your dog at the local club and have an afternoon's fun, most Whippets will take to racing with enthusiasm no matter how they are bred, but do remember the warning about having an acceptable five-generation pedigree.

Rearing and Training

The rearing of a racing puppy does not differ in any way from that of any other puppy. He needs to be properly fed to develop his full strength and stamina, and all dogs should be trained to behave in a socially acceptable manner.

WCRCh. She's A Bee (Our Girl Zippy).

However, it is possible to encourage a puppy's natural desire to chase by playing games with him in which he follows a piece of fur or rag pulled in front of him. The game must not last too long or it will have the opposite effect and he will become bored. It has been said that if you intend to race the Whippet he must not be allowed to chase live quarry or he will not be sufficiently enthusiastic about a lure. So chasing rabbits and squirrels should not form part of his exercise. Neither should these chasing games be played with another puppy, in case playing with his friend becomes his main object, thus encouraging him to try to play with the other dogs once he is on the track.

The puppy should be taken to the race-track from about six months of age and allowed to watch other dogs racing. If you ask permission you will be allowed to take him to stand near the traps at the start of trial racing, so that he becomes used to the noise of the trap doors banging open. You will also be allowed to walk him through the traps and stand him in a trap with the door closed. The more used to the noises of the track he becomes, the easier it will be when the time comes

138

for him to race. It is also advisable to buy a muzzle and let him wear it for a few moments from time to time, so that wearing a muzzle does not distract him during a race.

At nine months of age he will be allowed to trial. You will find that racing club officials are very helpful and will do all they can to ensure your puppy learns his job quickly and easily. The first trials will be hand-slipped up a straight track, and as soon as the pup is chasing the lure and running straight, he can progress to the traps. It is often best to start with the front of the trap up and the lure placed in front of the pup, so that although he can see it the moment it starts to move, he has to run through the trap to reach it. From here it is only a short step to being placed in the trap with the door closed and learning to come out as fast as possible to catch the lure.

From single-dog trials, he will progress to trials with two or three other dogs. He will be expected to start from the trap in front, in which case, dogs will be coming up behind him; or to run from one of the middle traps with dogs either side of him; and also from the outside trap so that he has to pass others. At no time must he turn his head or interfere with another dog, or it will be back to single-dog trials again. Once he is twelve months old, and has been passed by the trials manager, he will be ready to take his place in a proper race.

Do remember that even at twelve months he is still a baby, and do not be tempted to over-run him. He will not be fully mature until nearly two, and many a promising puppy has been ruined by too much racing at too early an age.

Training the Adult Racing Dog

The basis of all hard training for sporting Whippets is road-work. Opinions vary as to how much road-work is needed to get and keep a Whippet in top racing or coursing condition, but each dog must be treated as an individual and what suits one may not necessarily suit another. A brisk half hour in the morning, with a longer walk that includes a free gallop in the afternoon, would probably suit most dogs. A hand massage at the end of the walk helps to tone muscles and, if conditions are wet and muddy, feet should be washed in warm, salt water and dried thoroughly. Mud caked around the nail-beds can lead to inflammation and sore toes, and as the old grooms used to say, 'no feet, no horse'.

Feeding the Racing Dog

The diet for a racing dog is another area in which opinions are as many as stripes on a zebra. Every successful owner has his own special diet but, once again, common sense will tell you that a well-balanced diet of good-quality food which results in a gleaming coat and a lively dog, is the answer. Chapter 4 gives advice on diet for adult dogs.

Racing dogs are handicapped according to their weight, and there is always a tendency to think that by reducing the dog's weight and giving him half a yard's start on his opponent, you will increase his chance of winning. But dogs, like humans, have an ideal running weight and always run best at that weight. Reducing poundage could also reduce stamina, and speed on the final run in, so once you have found the weight at which the dog gives of his best, keep him on that amount of food. The use of 'go-faster' additives and potions is another source of argument amongst owners. Most do little or no good, and excessive use can upset the balance of any diet. Treat them with caution, though the addition of 'electrolytes' to the main meal just before and after violent exercise will replace minerals used during periods of great stress.

Lure Racing

This is the latest addition to the sporting activities of Whippets in Britain, although it has been a popular sport in North America and Europe for some years. It is sometimes called lure coursing, though it bears little relation to true coursing.

The lure is run in a large grass field, round a 550-yard (503-metre) track with several very sharp bends, said to represent the jinking of the hare. The fields are often quite undulating, so that the dogs have to run up and down hill, as well as on level ground. There is no marked track and the dogs have to follow the lure. Marks are given for agility, enthusiasm, follow, speed and endurance by two judges who are standing on a raised platform in the middle of the field. Each dog is judged separately and can choose to run alone rather than with another dog. The dogs run twice, once in the morning and again in the afternoon, and their points are added together.

The British Sighthound Field Association was started in 1989 by an enthusiastic group of Borzoi owners, headed by John Stears and Nicki Morgan. It is open, as the name suggests, to all dogs that fall within the sighthound category, i.e. Whippets Borzois, Salukis, Greyhounds, Deerhounds, Wolfhounds, Afghans, Basenjis, Ibizans, Pharoah Hounds and Sloughis. All the dogs taking part must be registered with the Kennel Club, and each breed runs separately. Greyhounds registered with the National Greyhound Coursing Club would also be accepted.

The first meeting was held, in pouring rain, on 2 April 1989 and the greatest number of entries at that and all subsequent meetings, have always been Whippets. The Deerhounds also put up a very good show, and it is certainly very interesting to see so many different breeds taking part.

Although lure racing is fun, it is also hazardous. The very sharp bends cause the faster dogs to over-run the lure, and there are the usual natural lumps and bumps found in fields. The pulleys are exposed and, although painted black to make them more easily seen, they have been known to cause injury to the dogs.

Neither does the present method of judging appear very precise. Timing is bound to cause difficulties when dogs are free to cut corners at will, and certainly it appears to be the stylish and not overly fast dogs that come out on top, but if you do not worry too much about points, and ask only for a thoroughly enjoyable day out, lure racing could be your sport.

12

Whippets Abroad

Europe

The Federation Cynologique Internationale (FCI), based in Belgium, governs pedigree dog activities in Europe. The Kennel Clubs of Europe, as well as those in Scandinavia, Japan, Mexico and South America, all belong to this organization.

The Breed Standard is that of the Kennel Club, but the maximum height for dogs is 51cm and for bitches 48cm (i.e. just over 20½ inches for dogs and just under 19 inches for bitches). The insistence on correct height means that a measuring stick is a common sight in Continental show rings, and in some countries dogs will not have their pedigree confirmed unless they have been officially measured and pronounced to be within the limit. Without such confirmation, the dogs can neither be bred from nor shown.

There is also much greater attention paid to specific details of the Standard, such as eye colour, pigmentation, ear carriage and dentition. Not only will a judge examine the dog's mouth for a correct bite, but he will also check that all pre-molars are present; a judge in the UK would probably check only for a correct bite. Such points as dark eyes and pigmentation might well be considered by an English judge to be of minor importance, as, under the Kennel Club Standard, he is allowed far more discretion, and would be more concerned with balance, type and movement.

The Continental style of judging results in a more uniform type of Whippet being exhibited, with less variation in type, size and quality than we see in the UK, but with perhaps fewer outstanding examples of the breed.

Judges under FCI rules have to give a written report on every dog, with a grading. These gradings are Excellent, Very Good, Good and a fourth category meaning more or less disqualification. The 'Excellent' grading indicates that the judge considers the dog of champion quality and, even if a dog is not placed in the first four in the class but gains this grade, the owner would be well pleased. The classification at shows is very limited in comparison with the number of classes available at UK shows. There are very few puppy classes except at the larger Breed Club Shows. Normally there are only Junior Classes, Open Classes and Champion Classes, together with Working Classes and various Breeders' Classes. The grading system does mean that in a large, strong class a judge is able to indicate how many dogs he considers to be of great merit; and in a weak class, though a dog wins a place, he might not have gained the sought-after 'Excellent'.

The Championship System

The systems under which European dogs obtain the title of Champion are very complicated. At each Championship Show, the winners in some of the classes, though not the Champion Class, compete for the CAC (Certificat d'Aptitude Championnat); which classes are eligible for the CAC varies from country to country. This is a national Champion Certificate and in most countries, a dog who wins four CACs will become a Champion of that country. The French Kennel Club insists that one of these must be either at the Paris Show or The National Breeders' Show and they also rule that a Whippet must hold a working certificate to prove that he can race.

Champions may not compete for the CAC and may only be entered in the Champion Class, from which they compete for the CACIB (Certificat d'Aptitude au Championnat International de Beauté) and Best of Breed. To become an International Champion, a dog must have won four CACIBs in three different countries, under three different judges, and there must be a minimum of twelve months between the first and third CACIB. One CACIB must have been gained in the country of residence, and an imported dog may count a Challenge Certificate gained in the country from which the breed originated.

All this means that although it might be easier to make up a national champion in most European countries (except perhaps in France with their insistence on a win at particular annual shows), the distances covered by those exhibitors with International Champions fill one with admiration for their enthusiasm and powers of endurance.

Racing

In most of Europe, the ability to race is officially recognized as being an important characteristic of the Whippet. In Holland, and in Germany particularly, breeding for racing has played a considerable part in Whippet development, and the dogs are presented in the ring in much harder condition than is often the case in the UK.

In order to become a French champion, not only does a dog have to win the CAC at either the Paris Show or the National Breeders' Show, but he has to hold a 'Certificat d'Aptitude à la Course' with a 'Très Bien' to show that he can race sufficiently fast to carry a 'Categorie B' grading. If the dog does not already hold such a certificate, he must produce one within two years or his title will be rescinded. Such a rule might cause considerable consternation in some British show kennels!

The Union Internationale des Club Levriers (UICL) organizes both Whippet showing and racing on the Continent. Most countries are members, and meetings are held throughout the year. These include an International Championship Meeting and various Open Meetings. One of the most prestigious awards for a European Whippet is the Schönheit and Rennleistung plaque for the dog who has combined the greatest success both on the race-track and in the show ring.

When the Whippet Club founded the WCRA in the UK, Mr Norman Odell, who was the Chairman, and Mrs Joanna Russell, the first Registrar of the Association, visited Holland to study the way in which the Dutch had organized their racing. As a result, the layout of the WCRA tracks is based on that used so successfully by the Dutch.

France

Whippets are a popular breed in France, and have been since the middle of the nineteenth century. The French Whippet Club was formed late in the 1940s, and now has approximately nine hundred members, not all of whom exhibit their dogs – many are only interested in racing while others have their Whippets solely as pets.

When exporting a dog to France, a breeder has to be very aware of the question of size but, despite this, some notable English exports have achieved success including Fr. Ch. Laguna Leonora and Fr. Ch. Martinsell Piquet, who both won well for their respective owners, the Comtesse de St Seine and the Comtesse de Bearne. Piquet, who proved exceptionally fast, broke the track record in France.

When Mrs Russell and Mrs Brown lost three of their brood bitches (including one of the very few black champions, Ch. Martinsell Grand Slam, and her dam) in a tragic accident, they were lent a bitch by the

Comtesse de Bearne. This bitch was imported, in whelp to a dog who carried their lost blood-line, and the puppies were born in quarantine. The puppies, one of which is the lovely fawn, Cliquot of Martinsell, remained in England, and the dam returned to her owner in France. This complicated and expensive operation enabled the Martinsell kennel to continue their carefully planned breeding programme.

Ex-patriot English breeders have also had an influence on French breeding. Lady Selway (Ballagan), Mrs Stancomb (Tinribs) and Mrs Mather (Dillwyn) all took their Whippets with them while residing in France for a number of years. They enjoyed much success while there, and now their blood-lines can be found in many European pedigrees.

Int. Ch. Neon of Nevedith was imported by M. Cappi for his Enfants de la Tramontane kennels, and this dog has proved his worth by both winning well and siring successful puppies.

Mme Claude Rebourg has imported several dogs from England, including Int. Ch. Demelza of Tamsmorna, (litter sister to the Cruft's Hound Group Winner, Ch. Jubilant Lady of Tygreen and Lowerdon), and Tamsmorna Rowella. Demelza was mated to another of her imports, Midsummer Knight at Chyton, and produced Int. Ch. Talk of the Town d'Escla; Rowella was mated to Ch. Statesman of Silkstone (imported into Holland by Frank Sampers of the Epicurian kennels). Many European champions are descended from these lines.

One of the largest breeders in France believes in being truly international. Mme Karen Mesavage of the Sac à Malices kennel has not only had notable success with Silkstone imports, but has brought in American blood-lines with her Int. Am. Ch. Itsme Autumn's Copper Glow, and a daughter of the top American sire, Ch. Plumcreek Chimney Swift. She even exported a French-bred bitch to the States, who became the dam of the aptly named Am. Ch. Itsme Pardon My French.

Holland

Although a small country, Holland hosts a number of large dog shows, and Whippets are a popular breed. As elsewhere on the Continent, racing plays a large part in Whippet activities and is probably one of the reasons why such emphasis is placed on correct size. The tallest dog may not exceed 20 inches (51 centimetres) and the bitch 19 inches (48 centimetres), so a Whippet that exceeds these limits is of little use to a Dutch breeder. Presentation and handling at the shows by some of the owners, whose real interest lies in the speed of their dog, may not be of the high standard found in England, but the dogs are certainly in very hard, fit condition.

Those dogs from primarily show kennels are of very high standard indeed and can and do enjoy much success all over Europe. The Samoems kennel of Tim Teillers, which is one of the most consistently successful Whippet kennels anywhere in the world, is based on Wingedfoot dogs imported some years ago. Later Mr Teillers imported Shalfleet stock and he has now added some American blood-lines. The Samoems' dogs are of a consistent type, with good bone and very sound on the move. They have dominated the show scene for many years, both in Holland and elsewhere on the Continent. Mr Teiller's partner, René Matheewsen, judges several hound breeds on the Continent, and has awarded Challenge Certificates in the UK.

Some years ago, Mrs Barbara Wilton-Clark of the Shalfleet kennel imported a brindle dog, Samoems Silent Knight, who was a son of Shalfleet Sylvine, a bitch whom she had exported to Mr Teillers. Silent Knight became the first imported dog to become a UK champion and, in turn, he sired champions in this country.

The Sylvan Dwelling Whippets of Lank Bos and Coos Huijsen are also very successful on the Continent. Their kennels are based on the imported bitch Shalfleet Sylvine, hence their prefix.

Frank Sampers imported two new blood-lines with the parti-coloured Int. Ch. Dondelayo Paint Tin and the mainly white Int. Ch. Statesman of Silkstone. Paint Tin was the son of Ch. Dondelayo Buckaroo, and Statesman was by Ch. Topall Newbold Miguel. Both have won well, but Statesman, in particular, has proved an excellent sire and has been used as far afield as France and Germany.

Scandinavia

According to Bo Bengtson, the Swedish writer, judge, exhibitor and acknowledged expert on all matters to do with sighthounds, pedigree dogs are more popular in Scandinavia than anywhere else in the world. Registrations with the four national kennel clubs, Denmark, Finland, Norway and Sweden, vary between one hundred and one hundred and fifty thousand each year, which is an astonishing number when one considers the relatively small population of these countries.

Until the 1950s, very few Whippets figured amongst these registrations and even now only about six hundred are registered annually, at least half of these being in Sweden. At present the only Whippet breed club in Scandinavia is the Swedish Whippet Club

(Svenska Whippetklubben), which was founded in 1976. This club holds several regional shows each year, as well as the marvellous national show at Skokloster Castle. Skokloster weekend has become a world event, with the prestigious Sighthound Club Show being held the same weekend. The fairy-tale setting with the old castle forming the backdrop, an entry of many of Europe's top sighthounds and famous international judges presiding, make it a weekend to remember for visitors.

The first important Whippet kennel was started in Norway as early as 1937, when Mrs Salvensen brought over Tiptree dogs from England, to which she later added Wingedfoot and Allways bloodlines. The Brenna kennels are now owned by Mrs Espeland, who imported the brindle and white Int. Ch. Dondelayo Jonty, who was so successful as a sire that many more Dondelayo dogs were exported to Scandinavia by Mrs Anne Knight.

Imported stock has played an important role in Scandinavia. Some of the early imports, such as Ch. Robmaywin Starshine of Allways, were of solid fawn breeding, but many of the later dogs were more brightly coloured and are responsible for the predominance of brindle and white parti-colours now seen in this part of Europe.

Mr Bengtson, though he bred relatively few litters, imported several very important sires into Sweden, which have had a great influence on the breed throughout Scandinavia. The first of these was Int. Ch. Laguna Locomite, probably the top-winning Whippet of all time in Sweden, and the second was Int. Ch. Laguna Leader, who sired twenty-five Scandinavian champions. Leader was by Ch. Laguna Ligonier, and his dam was litter sister to Am. Ch. Laguna Lucky Lad, who had such an influence on American Whippets. Mr Bengtson then brought in Int. Ch. Badgewood Mark Twain and Int. Ch. Shalfleet Starbuck. His most important import, however, was in 1971 when Mrs Molly Garrish allowed him to have Ch. Fleeting Flamboyant. Despite winning eleven Challenge Certificates and being top Whippet in 1967, Flamboyant's potential as a sire was not realized in England, and Mrs Garrish believed that he might be more appreciated in Scandinavia. There, in the expert hands of Mr Bengtson, Flamboyant ended his first year as one of the top dogs of all breeds. The great British all-round judge and dog man, Bobby James, wrote in the weekly journal *Our Dogs* that Flamboyant 'to a certain degree revolutionized the breed in Sweden', and he has certainly left his print on the type of Whippet being shown in that country today.

The willingness of Scandinavian breeders to import good dogs from abroad has resulted in a very wide gene pool on which to draw for future breeding programmes. The quality of their Whippets is very high. From a study of the excellent yearbook produced by the Swedish Whippet Club, the winning dogs appear to be of the highly coloured brindle and white parti-coloured type, and there does not seem to be the same insistence on correct size as in other parts of Europe.

Racing was not introduced into Sweden until early in 1970, when Mr & Mrs Permo of the Per-Mobile kennels set up the first track. It is now a very popular sport but does not hold as important a place in the life of the breed as it does in Germany, Holland and France. A champion does not have to hold a working certificate, as in France, nor is there any form of official title for a racing champion, as there is in Germany. Perhaps it is for this reason that size has been allowed to creep upwards?

The Rest of Europe

Whippets are to be found all over Europe, with many exported dogs from England helping to enlarge the possibilities for breeding sound stock of good breed type. Int. Champions Shalfleet Pollyanna, Laguna Lancelot and Laguna Lady Lightfoot were very successful for their respective owners, Mrs Ranft and Mrs Gut of Switzerland. In Austria, there are dogs going back to Int. Ch. Dreamland of Test, together with later additions from Newbold and Courthill, while in Belgium, Champions Glenbervie Steelsword and Garnstones Marna are behind the du Panisel breeding of Jean Cartier.

Italy has attracted a whole string of top English champions. Mrs Anne Knight sent Ch. Denhills Delectabelle to the Baroness Renai della Rena soon after the bitch won the Challenge Certificate at Cruft's, and Delectabelle was only the forerunner of many successful imports into Italy. Probably the greatest number of English dogs have been shown by Mauro Carpone of the Almaglo kennels. He has owned English Champions, Novacroft Starbright, Glenbervie White Frost, Savilepark Sweet Harmony and other top-winning dogs. The Almaglo kennels have won well in Europe and Mme Bourdin's lovely fawn bitch, Int. Ch. Almaglo Norcis, whom Mrs Mary Lowe made Junior World Champion in Amsterdam in 1985, was bred by Mr Carpone. Norcis, by Ch. Samarkand Sigma out of Ch. Silkstone Spun Silk, is entirely Dondelayo and Oakbark breeding.

The only country in Europe with very few English imports is West Germany, who breed very successfully from old German lines or from those of neighbouring countries. One might suppose that with so many of the best English blood-lines already available, it is unnecessary to go to the trouble and expense of importing your own!

It will be most interesting to see if, in the years to come, with the advent of the Channel Tunnel and the changes that this feat of engineering will bring, dogs from the Continent will play a greater part in the plans of English breeders.

America

Although the modern Whippet emerged in England, the first Whippet ever to be registered with a Kennel Club was a dog named Jack Dempsey. He was registered with the American Kennel Club in 1888 under the heading 'Miscellaneous'. The breed was not recognized by the English Kennel Club until 1890. Six years later, six Whippets were shown at the most important dog show in America, the Westminster Kennel Club Show, and by 1904 the dog Imperial Deodora Pride had become the first American Champion Whippet.

Many of the leading American kennels based their breeding on imported English stock, and the same names are far back in the pedigrees of winning Whippets in both countries. Bitches must have been imported to America already in whelp to famous English champions, as Ch. Shirley Wanderer and Watford Bon appear as sires of some of the early Whippets. The famous Meander kennel of the two Misses Shearer was based on an imported dog, Ch. Sandbrilliant of Meander, and their home-bred Ch. Syndicate of Meander, herself a daughter of the imported Ch. Towyside Teasle. The equally important kennels of Mrs Anderson (Mardormere), Mrs Newcombe (Pennyworth) and Mrs Wear (Stoney Meadows) imported top-class English dogs with great success. Ch. Laguna Lucky Lad, Ch. Greenbrae Barn Dance, Ch. Courtenay Fleetfoot of Pennyworth, Ch. Fleeting Falcon of Pennyworth, Ch. Tantivvey Diver of Pennyworth and more recently Ch. Charmoll Clansman, Ch. Nevedith Up Town Guy and Ch. Hardknott Maestro of Bohem, are all exported UK champions whose progeny have contributed greatly to the American show scene.

Before he left England, Up Town Guy served only two bitches, one of which was Chilka Dairy Maid. Fortunately, Mr and Mrs Newton chose two bitch puppies from this litter, one of which became the famous Ch. Nutshell of Nevedith (*see* page 91). Up Town Guy is now an American champion and is siring top-winning stock.

Maestro's co-owner, Bo Bengtson, also acquired a young, virtually

149

unshown dog, Chatwig Chinook, who had been imported into America. This youngster is now an American champion and is siring top-winning stock, and so the tradition goes on.

The American Type

Although a pure-bred Whippet is a Whippet in whatever country he is bred, each country favours a different type, and these differences can be traced back to the variations in the Breed Standard laid down by the respective Kennel Clubs. The American Standard varies from that of the United Kingdom in several ways. The main divergence is in the height, front and shoulder construction, and in the eye colour and pigmentation.

The American Standard has as its height specification 19 to 22 inches for dogs and 18 to 21 inches for bitches, with a disqualification for any dog one half inch above or below these heights. The UK Standard lays down an 'ideal' height of between 18 and 20 inches for dogs and $17\frac{1}{2}$–$18\frac{3}{4}$ inches for bitches, with no disqualification clauses at all, and the decision is left to the discretion of the judge.

The American Standard also calls for a dark eye with the pigmentation around the eye complete, and lists upright ears as incorrect and to be severely penalized. The UK Standard asks only for bright, oval-shaped eyes with an alert expression and for ears to be small, fine in texture and 'rose shaped'.

These variations in the Standards have led to a difference in the type of Whippet that can win in the ring. This is compounded by the fact that the vast majority of American shows are judged by all-rounders and not specialist judges; in Britain, only a comparatively few all-round judges award Challenge Certificates in Whippets. The tall, elegant eye-catching brindle and white parti-colour, with dark eyes and perfect ear-carriage, predominates and is, in general, the Whippet that does the winning in the show ring of America.

The Championship System

The system of making up a champion in America is totally different from that in this country. It is based on a complicated system of points, which is revised annually by the American Kennel Club according to the competition in each breed and region. Championship points are not gained by competing against other champion dogs. Champions are shown in the Specials Class and compete for Best of Breed only.

A dog must gain fifteen points for his title, with at least two major wins, that is wins at shows where there were sufficient entries to warrant three to five points being allotted. This means that he may neither have met nor defeated another champion on the road to his title.

The result of this system is that between one and two hundred new Whippet champions are made up every year, and the title does not carry the same status that it does in Europe. Far more importance is paid to Group and Best in Show wins, whereas in this country such awards are regarded as the icing on the cake, and the dog is judged by the number of Challenge Certificates he gains.

Racing in America

Between the two World Wars, Whippet racing was a large and flourishing sport in America. It was conducted on a lavish scale unknown in England, with six dog races being run several times a week on specially built tracks, with betting and prize money, very much as Greyhound racing operates today. Many of the dogs taking part were bred from imported stock and some were even wire-coated, as were their early English counterparts.

By the 1950s, however, racing appears to have virtually died out, certainly on the professional level of the 1920s and 1930s. A few enthusiasts continued and gradually the breed clubs, notably The Whippet Breeders' Association of Maryland, encouraged those holding shows to put on exhibition racing. This led to a revival of interest in the sport and many show kennels began to aim for dual-purpose dogs. In 1958, official Whippet racing started again under the supervision of The American Whippet Club. The dogs now run under Official Rules and Regulations for National Whippet Racing. In 1966, the American Whippet Club inaurugated the Award of Racing Merit Certificate programme. This award is very highly prized and dogs use the initials ARM on their pedigrees. It is calculated on a points system very similar to that used for awarding a Show Champion title.

Coursing

Open-Field Coursing Coursing was as common in the United States as in most countries with wide open spaces, plenty of hares and dogs fast enough to catch them. It did not become organized, however, until 1961 when an advisory committee on sighthound coursing was set up. Now it is possible for a Whippet to gain the Award of Coursing Merit and use the initials ACM after his name. Once again, this title is based on a points system similar to that used in the show ring. The Kennel Club in London does not recognize any coursing title and, no matter how many Open Stakes a dog may win, he will not be entitled to a coursing title. Only the enthusiasts can tell you how special an English coursing dog may be.

American Lure Coursing   The American Sighthound Field Association has governed the running of this sport since 1972, and its rules and methods have been copied by the British Sighthound Field Association in England. The dogs chase an electric lure around a field with several twists and turns and are alloted marks for the way they run. Although it is called lure coursing in America, it really bears much more resemblance to racing. If a dog gains the required number of points under rules, he may carry the initials LCM (Lure Courser of Merit) after his name. Well-known show dogs frequently win at the lure course trials, and there was even one show champion, Ch. Flippet's Appraxin Marshall, LCM, who was the top lure courser of 1978.

Canada

Whippets bred in Canada are registered with the Canadian Kennel Club, which does not have quite the same rules and regulations as its American counterpart. There are also differences in the Breed Standard between America, the United Kingdom and Canada. Owing to the variation in the system of points, a dog may not transfer points gained in Canada, towards an American Championship title, or points gained in America to Canada. Each Kennel Club, however, recognizes the registrations of the other, and it is only when a dog becomes permanently resident in one country that his registration has to be transferred. Dogs living near the border, therefore, can move backwards and forwards to shows without any technical problems.

Canadian breeders probably import more from England than the Americans do, but they also bring in stock from America, and many Canadian and American pedigrees carry the same blood-lines. They have even reversed the trend and, in 1987, Mrs Wilton-Clark of the Shalfleet kennels imported the American and Canadian Champion Lorricbrook Runaway from Max Magder's kennels, and the dog very quickly became a triple champion. Mr Magder had imported Ch. Dondelayo Buccaneer some years before and made him into Canada's top Whippet, and sire of many champions in both Canada and America.

Several Whippet breeders from the UK have emigrated to Canada with their Whippets, and the Sakonnet, Mispickel, Ringdove, Boarley and Padneyhill prefixes are as well known there as they are here.

The Working Dog in Canada

Whippet racing in Canada is run under the auspices of the American Whippet Club, with the opportunity to win the same ARM title.

Lure coursing started in Canada in 1976 and is organized by the Canadian Sighthound Field Association, with a similar system to that of the American Association. As in America, there are many show winners taking part in this sport, which once again proves the versatility of the breed.

While it may be true that it is easier for an American or Canadian Whippet to gain a title of some kind, either in the show ring, on the track or in the field, it does indicate a properly appreciative view of the working dog by their respective Kennel Clubs. Many of the faults which creep into breeds in England, which are judged solely by their performance in the show ring, might become less prevalent and give less cause for concern, if there was some form of official encouragement given to owners who also use their dogs for the purpose for which they are designed.

13

Famous Dogs

Top-Winning Show Champions 1980–90
Based on the number of Challenge Certificates won during the year.

1980

Dog:	Ch. Samoems Silent Knight of Shalfleet
DoB:	22.8.77
Colour:	Brindle
Sire:	Ch. Samoems Scorpion
Dam:	Shalfleet Sylvine
Breeder:	Mr T. Teiller
Owner:	Mrs B. Wilton-Clark

Bitch:	Ch. Jubilant Lady of Tygreen and Lowerdon
DoB:	1.12.76
Colour:	Fawn
Sire:	UK and SA Ch. Beseeka Knight Errant of Silkstone
Dam:	Oakbark Miniver
Breeder:	Miss J. Smith
Owner:	Mr and Mrs H. Marshall

1981

Dog:	Ch. Novacroft Madrigal
DoB:	8.3.79
Colour:	Brindle/White
Sire:	Ch. Charmoll McTavish
Dam:	Novacroft Starlet
Breeder:	Mrs D. Gardner
Owner:	Mrs P. Gilmour and Mrs F. Broadbent

Bitch:	Ch. Laura Love of Lounell
DoB:	13.2.78
Colour:	Fawn/White
Sire:	Ch. Dondelayo Buckaroo

Dam: Dondelayo Lauretta
Breeder: Owner
Owner: Mr G. Morris

1982

Dog: Ch. Shalfleet Silent Wish
DoB: 21.6.80
Colour: Fawn
Sire: Ch. Samoems Silent Knight of Shalfleet
Dam: Shalfleet Storyteller
Breeder: Owner
Owner: Mrs B. Wilton-Clark

Bitch: Ch. Martinsell Grand Slam
DoB: 17.1.81
Colour: Black
Sire: Ch. Poaching Black Jack
Dam: Martinsell Cache-Cache
Breeder: Owners
Owners: Mrs C. Brown and Mrs E. Russell

and

Bitch: Ch. Lowglen Blue Mink at Dennydene
DoB: 15.7.80
Colour: Brindle/White
Sire: Ch. Novacroft Madrigal
Dam: Ch. Lowglen Singing Bede
Breeder: Mr F. Nicholas
Owner: Mrs K. Sedgley

1983

Dog: Ch. Cottonmere Monty of Oakbark
DoB: 22.6.80
Colour: Fawn/White
Sire: Oakbark Mr Blue
Dam: Ribblesmere Xmas Caroll
Breeder: Miss D. Greenwood
Owner: Mr and Mrs D. Meakin

Bitch: Ch. Selinko Another Lady
DoB: 29.8.81
Colour: Fawn

Sire:	Marlins Dusty Miller of Iniskelltr
Dam:	Silver Bambi of Selinko
Breeder:	Owners
Owners:	Mr and Mrs B. Kennett

1984

Dog:	Ch. Nevedith Paper Weight
DoB:	15.2.82
Colour:	Brindle/White
Sire:	Nevedith Merry Monarch
Dam:	Whitbarrow Mini Mist
Breeder:	Owner
Owner:	Mrs E. W. Newton-Reid

| Bitch: | Ch. Selinko Another Lady (*see* 1983) |

1985

Dog:	Ch. Nimrodel Wanderer
DoB:	6.12.83
Colour:	Fawn
Sire:	Nimrodel Dragoon
Dam:	Nimrodel Wanton
Breeder:	Mrs I. H. Lowe
Owner:	Mrs J. Minns

| Bitch: | Ch. Selinko Another Lady (*see* 1983) |

1986

Dog	Ch. Welstar Royal Mint
DoB:	20.8.77
Colour:	Fawn
Sire:	Ch. Nimrodel Wiverton
Dam:	Ch. Welstar Minted Model
Breeder:	Mrs L. Jones
Owner:	Mr and Mrs G. Hempstock

Bitch:	Ch. Lowglen Magic Moments
DoB:	20.11.82
Colour:	Fawn
Sire:	Ch. Carmodian Tawny Knight of Hutaka
Dam:	Ch. Lowglen Singing Bede
Breeder:	Owner
Owner:	Mr F. Nicholas

and

Bitch:	Ch. Oakbark Mary Rose
DoB:	4.9.83
Colour:	Fawn
Sire:	Ch. Oakbark Middleman
Dam:	Ch. Oakbark Must Love
Breeders:	Owners
Owners:	Mr and Mrs D. Meakin

1987

Dog:	Ch. Capo Di Monte
DoB:	4.9.85
Colour:	Fawn/White
Sire:	Ch. Allgarth Atlantis at Sagewood
Dam:	Oakbark May Queen
Breeder:	Owner
Owner:	Mrs M. Moore

Bitch:	Ch. Baldrey Limited Edition of Juneric
DoB:	9.1.86
Colour:	Fawn
Sire:	Ch. Nimrodel Wanderer
Dam:	Baldrey Silent Willow
Breeder:	Mrs J. White
Owner:	Mrs J. Minns

1988

Dog:	Ch. Nimrodel Wanderer (*see* 1985)
Bitch:	Ch. Baldry Limited Edition of Juneric (*see* 1987)

1989

Dog:	Ch. Nimrodel Wanderer (*see* 1985)

and

Dog:	Ch. Tilegreen Tornado
DoB:	17.6.87
Colour:	Brindle
Sire:	Ch. Carmodian Tawny Knight of Hutaka
Dam:	Tilegreen Misty Morning
Breeder:	Mrs J. Smith
Owner:	Mrs M. Blanks

Bitch: Ch. Nutshell of Nevedith
DoB: 22.1.87
Colour: Brindle/White
Sire: Ch. Nevedith Up Town Guy
Dam: Chilka Dairy Maid
Breeders: Mr and Mrs J. Barker
Owner: Mrs E. Newton-Reid

The record for the number of CCs won is held by Mrs Newton-Reid's
Ch. Nutshell of Nevedith with 36 CCs (*see* page 91). She superseded Mr
and Mrs Kennett's Ch. Selinko Another Lady, who won 25 CCs.

Mrs Minn's Ch. Nimrodel Wanderer holds the record for dogs with
22 CCs, followed by Ch. Welstar Royal Mint with 19.

Top Stud Dogs

The breed record holder for the number of champions sired is held by
Ch. Laguna Ligonier, eleven of whose progeny became champions.

Ch. Wingedfoot Marksman of Allways, Ch. Pilot Officer Prune and
Ch. Akeferry Jimmy all sired ten champions. Ch. Cockrow Tarquogan
of Glenbervie, Ch. Dondelayo Buckaroo and Ch. Lowglen Newbold
Cavalier had nine champion offspring, whilst Ch. Bellavisa Barry had
eight.

There does not seem to be the same dominance by one dog shown
in the pedigrees of champions at the present time, and there are many
well-known stud dogs with two, three or four champion progeny.
However, both Ch. Nimrodel Ruff and Ch. Charmoll McTavish have
sired six UK champions, as well as overseas champions, which is a
remarkable record.

Top Coursing Whippets 1980–90

The names in this table have been compiled from the meticulous records of Major Antony Loch since 1980. It is only since that date that
records of the results of each season's coursing in all four clubs have
been kept and it is for that reason that the dogs listed here have been
restricted to those running after 1980. There were many excellent
Whippets coursing before 1980 and I am sure that there will be many
more names to add in the years to come. The names are in alphabeti-
cal order rather than in any particular order of merit.

Ch. Nimrodel Ruff (right) and Ch. Nimrodel Wiveton (left), two very influential sires. Both dogs were capable of giving an excellent account of themselves in the coursing field, and their blood-lines are behind not only show champions, but many coursing winners.

Dog: Ballagan Rouge Dragon
Owner: Hon. Mrs Cabbell-Manners
Breeder: Lady Selway
Sire: Ch. Samoems Silent Knight of Shalfleet
Dam: Ballagan Fanfare

Dog: Ch. Chyton Copy-Press
Owner: Mrs S. A. Rawlings
Breeder: Owner
Sire: Moonlake Master Copy of Chyton
Dam: Sweet Briar

Dog: Greywhip I'm Quickest Too
Owner: Mrs L. Robinson
Breeder: Owner
Sire: Greywhip I'm Quickest
Dam: Culverstreet Calvados

Dog: Jealous Hussy
Owner: Mr J. Hamilton
Breeder: Owner
Sire: Laguna Larkin
Dam: Jest Harmony

Dog: Jimanica Jacinda
Owner: Mrs V. Hill
Breeder: Owner
Sire: Laguna Lingay
Dam: Highfield Lady Lizzie

Dog: Jimanica Jet Run
Owner: Mrs V. Hill
Breeder: Mrs A. Spencer-Thomas
Sire: Ch. Sound Barrier
Dam: Katie Jubilee Lady

Dog: Jimanica Jungle Bunny
Owner: Mrs A. Spencer-Thomas
Breeder: Owner
Sire: Ch. Sound Barrier
Dam: Katie Jubilee Lady

Dog: June Honeymoon
Owner: Mrs J. Allen
Breeder: Mr J. Hamilton
Sire: Maximillian of Chyton
Dam: Jealous Hussy

Dog: Laguna Black Larmite
Owner: Mrs L. Bond-Gunning
Breeder: Mrs D. McKay
Sire: Wymere Black Casanova
Dam: Laguna Black Lupina

Dog: Laguna Leader
Owner: Mrs D. McKay
Breeder: Owner
Sire: Laguna Leezer
Dam: Laguna Larissa

Dog: Maximillian of Chyton
Owner: Mrs S. A. Rawlings
Breeder: Mrs C. Dowsett
Sire: Chancerick Kaspar
Dam: Layer Albertine

Dog: Ch. Sound Barrier
Owner: Miss S. Baird
Breeder: Owner
Sire: Ch. Waycross Wishing Star
Dam: Sunday Best

Dog: Stubwood Baroness
Owner: Mr Sandell
Breeder: Owner
Sire: Laguna Larkin
Dam: Laguna Lylybet

Dog: Summersway Lark
Owner: Mrs P. Stenborg
Breeder: Mrs H. Worsfold
Sire: Kiwi of Summersway
Dam: Summersway Nightingale

Dog: Tamilinden Tilia of Culverstreet
Owner: Mr V. Granger
Breeder: Miss C. Dalton
Sire: Ch. Sound Barrier
Dam: Heffle Gypsy Moth

Dog: Terichline Fidelius
Owner: Mrs C. Dowsett
Breeder: Owner
Sire: Maximillian of Chyton
Dam: Haraiser Huntress

Dog: Wirrawon Touchtoes
Owner: Miss J. Fisher
Breeder: Owner
Sire: Wirrawon Sirrino
Dam: Haraiser Hell's Angel of Wirrawon

WHIPPETS

Summary of Results

		STAKES RUN	WON	QUALIFYING FINALS RU	DIV	TOTAL	COURSES RUN	TIMES BEATEN	RATIO	POINTS
Good Puppies										
Hungryhall Bashful	d	4	–	2	–	2	9	4	2:1	8
Hungryhall Benjamin	d	5	2	1	1	4	11	1	11:1	18
Terichline Kestrel	b	9	1	2	1	4	17	6	3:1	16
Top Dogs										
Dogs										
Jimanica Jaguar*		14	4	–	–	4	21	8	2½:1	15
Jimanica Jensen*		6	1	1	1	3	11	3	4:1	12
Stableyard Boynden Bugler**		6	1	1	1	3	12	3	4:1	12
Bitches										
Ashley Running Wild**		7	1	2	–	3	15	5	3:1	12
Chyton Bonne Chance**		10	5	1	1	7	25	4	6:1	38
Jazz Razzmatazz Jimanica		13	4	–	–	4	20	9	2:1	20
June Honeymoon*		8	2	–	2	4	13	3	4:1	15
Laguna Black Larmite*		11	2	1	–	3	18	9	2:1	10
Moondyne Snipe**		8	1	3	–	4	17	6	3:1	12
Moviestar Madam**		13	3	2	2	7	26	8	3:1	25
Setphair Eurythmic*		14	3	3	2	8	28	7	4:1	32
Tamalinden Tilia of Culverstreet*		8	2	1	–	3	14	5	3:1	12
Terichline Juno**		13	3	2	–	5	21	7	3:1	21

* Previous Top Dog
** Good Puppy last season

Opposite is the summary for the 1989/90 season, showing the complicated system devised by Major Loch, and used by him when calculating his results.

Major Loch prefers to call puppies 'good' rather than list them as 'top dogs', as he feels that a Whippet must prove himself over more than one season. A 'top dog' is an adult who has run well in one season, whereas the dogs listed above have proved themselves over several seasons.

It remains to be seen if any of the six young dogs starred with can continue to run well enough in their next two seasons to join in the exceptional category above.

Leading Coursing Sires 1980–90

In the early years of the decade, the leading sire of coursing winners was undoubtedly Lady Horsborough-Porter's Silver Whisper, with Mrs Simmond's Ch. Waycross Wishing Star, Mrs Meek's Chancerick Koh-i-nor and Miss Hawthorn's Ch. Deepridge Mintmaster also very successful.

As the whippets by these dogs became older, Laguna Larkin (also very successful as a racing sire), dominated the scene for a few years, until Miss Baird's Ch. Sound Barrier and Maximillian of Chyton began to make their mark.

Tragically, Ch. Sound Barrier died early, but his numerous progeny continue to run very well. Maximillian's offspring are also well to the fore, and his son Terichline Fidelius has become a leading sire in his own right. Mrs McKay's Laguna Leader is producing some highly successful stock, as is Mrs Minn's Ch. Nimrodel Wanderer.

Famous Whippet Club Racing Champions

This list has been compiled with the aid of Mrs Daphne Kitchen and Mrs Margaret Baker, both of whom have served on the Committee of the WCRA for many years.

It would not be possible to list all the racing champions, any more than it would be possible to list all bench champions, but the following might be considered to have run exceptionally well over several seasons. They are listed alphabetically rather than in any particular order of merit.

KC Name: Blue Frost Lady
Racing Name: Nippy Girl
Owner: Mr and Mrs Cairns
Sire: WCRCh. Chancerick Kondor
Dam: Leapaway Leading Lady

KC Name: Carlstream Silver Lagoon
Racing Name: Sierra
Owner: Mrs P. Billingham
Sire: Laguna Larkin
Dam: Firebrace Quality Lady

KC Name: Caroles Blue Zelda
Racing Name: Peanut
Owner: Mr H. Field
Sire: WCRCh. Mystic Pepe
Dam: Caroles Black Ranee

KC Name: Casaloma Cassandra
Racing Name: Beetle
Owner: Mr C. England
Sire: Knockaphrumpa
Dam: Selbrook Siona

KC Name: Casaloma Misty Morn
Racing Name: Sailor
Owner: Mrs M. Baker
Sire: Son of Sid
Dam: Carnival Queen

KC Name: Casaloma Sea Pigeon
Racing Name: Jolly
Owner: Mrs M. Baker
Sire: Laguna Larkin
Dam: Charminster Flete of Casaloma

KC Name: Chancerick Kondor
Racing Name: Kondor
Owner: Mrs S. MacDonald
Sire: Ebzan Noudini Bey Noir
Dam: Chancerick Nimrodel Rosefinch

164

KC Name: Firebrace Quality Lady
Racing Name: Silver Stream
Owner: Mrs P. Billingham
Sire: Walkabout Woodwasp
Dam: Michails Bitter Queen

KC Name: Glad Tidings
Racing Name: Earlswood Glad Tidings
Owner: Mr and Mrs Cutler
Sire: WCRCh. Bills Beano
Dam: Jay for Julie

KC Name: Hint of Mint
Racing Name: Little Minx
Owner: Mr and Mrs Evans
Sire: Pippawood Marbled White
Dam: Papedaro Camellia

KC Name: Jacks Boy
Racing Name: Jacks Boy
Owner: Mr J. Rees
Sire: Clipper of Hardknott
Dam: Natanis Serene

KC Name: Joater Misty
Racing Name: White Wizard
Owner: Major and Mrs Coates
Sire: Tarbuck of Heatherpard
Dam: Chinnor Oracle

KC Name: Kemerton Lauraine
Racing Name: Pippa
Owner: Mrs D. Kitchen
Sire: Laguna Larkin
Dam: Kemerton Honeymoon

KC Name: Madishan Moonlake
Racing Name: Luke
Owner: Miss G. Robertson
Sire: Ch. Laguna Light Lagoon
Dam: Madishan Moonflower

KC Name: Our Girl Zippy
Racing Name: She's a B
Owner: Mr F. Foley
Sire: Riversmeet Kittiwake
Dam: Goodad Breeze Along

KC Name: Pippawood Mountain Apollo
Racing Name: Always Skint
Owner: Miss L. Bailey
Sire: Kemerton Polo
Dam: Kemerton Khaki

KC Name: Pippawood Spanish Festoon
Racing Name: Zippa
Owner: Mr J. Rosser
Sire: WCRCh. Mountain Apollo
Dam: WCRCh. Kemerton Lauraine

KC Name: Sootican Princess
Racing Name: Picketty Witch
Owner: Mr T. Peart
Sire: Abbotts Anny Pride
Dam: WCRCh. Vangirl

KC Name: Tell um Straight
Racing Name: Striker
Owner: Mr and Mrs Legg
Sire: Pippawood Marbled White
Dam: Papedaro Camellia

KC Name: Vangirl
Racing Name: Vangirl
Owner: Mrs J. Keable
Sire: Shalfleet Saga
Dam: April Rose

Leading Racing Sires

Dog: Blue Streak of Ocklynge
Owner: Mrs P. Gaitskell

Dog: WCRCh. Carlstream Fire Star
Owner: Mr and Mrs Fuller

Dog: WCRCh. Casaloma Sea Pigeon
Owner: Mrs M. Baker

Dog: WCRCh. Chancerick Kondor
Owner: Mrs S. MacDonald

Dog: Laguna Larkin
Owner: Dr W. Adams

Dog: WCRCh. Pippawood Marbled White
Owner: Mr R. Jury

Dog: WCRCh. Pippawood Mountain Apollo
Owner: Miss L. Bailey

Dog: Tarbuck of Heatherpard
Owner: Mrs H. Tester

Appendix 1

UK Breed Clubs and Whippet Rescue

Below are the names and addresses of Whippet breed club secretaries in the UK. Telephone numbers are given where possible.

The East Anglian Whippet Club
Mrs G. Sage
The Pightle
Ringstead Road
Sedgeford
Nr Hunstanton
Norfolk PE36 5NQ
Tel. 0485 70936

The Midland Whippet Club
Mrs W. Spencer
15 Mill Lane
Toft
Cambridgeshire CB3 7RW
Tel. 022 026 2734

The National Whippet
  Association
Mr M. Howgate
21 Heatherdown Road
West Moors
Wimborne
Dorset
Tel. 0202 871775

The North Eastern Whippet
  Society
Mrs M. Gardener
83 Ewesley Road
High Barns
Sunderland
Tyne & Wear SR4 7RJ

The Northern Counties
  Whippet Club
Mr J. Parkinson
16 Memory Close
Freckleton
Lancashire PR4 1YS
Tel. 0772 635590

The Northern Ireland Whippet
  Club
Mrs M. Sloan
41 Thornleigh Park
Lisburn
Co Antrim
Northern Ireland BT28 2DD

The South Yorkshire Whippet
   Club
Mrs D. Bradshaw
129 Musgrave Crescent
Shirecliffe
Sheffield S5 7DR
Tel. 0742 385 502

The Whippet Club
Mr D. Mayger
Stoneways
32 Amersham Road
High Wycombe
Buckinghamshire HP13 6QU
Tel. 0494 23372

The Whippet Club of Scotland
Mrs J. McLeod
12 Livingstone Terrace
Dunlop
Ayrshire
Tel 0560 82446

The Whippet Club of Wales
Mrs J. Poole
25 Bampton Road
Llanrumney
Cardiff CF3 9SE
Tel. 0222 799819

Listed below are the three main Whippet rescue associations:

East Anglian Whippet Club
   Rescue
Mrs H. Fielden
The Cottage
Saltney Gate
Saracens Head
Lincolnshire
Tel. 0406 25170

J. R. Whippet Rescue
L. A. & B. R. Hunt
Joint Secretaries
Merry Boys Lodge
Merry Boys Lane
Cliffe Woods
Kent
Tel. 0634 220473

J. R. Whippet Rescue
Miss J. Fisher
(Treasurer)
9 Hatherley Road
Sidcup
Kent DA14 4BJ
Tel. 081 300 1339 or 081 300 9561

Appendix 2

Whippet Racing and Coursing Clubs

The secretaries of the four coursing clubs may be contacted through:

Miss S. Baird
Secretary of the National Whippet Coursing Club
Wyke Cottage
Queens Road
Crowborough
East Sussex
Tel. 0892 964617

Listed below are the secretaries of the racing clubs affiliated to the Whippet Club Racing Association:

Andover & District WRC
Mrs J. Keable
16 The Drove
Andover
Hampshire SP10 3DL

Dosthill Pedigree WRC
Mrs M. Mott
9 Main Street
Swepstone
Leicestershire

East Anglian WRC
Mr K. Spooner
3 Anderson Avenue
Chelmsford
Essex CM1 2BZ

East Sussex WRC
Miss S. Ireland
17 Penn Gardens
Ashington
Pulborough
West Sussex

Gloucester WRC
Mrs C. Mardle
21 Foxwell Drive
Hucclecote
Gloucestershire GL3 3LF

Harvel Pedigree WRC
Miss J. Fisher
9 Hatherly Road
Sidcup
Kent DR14 4BH

Maidstone & Mid-Kent WRC
Mrs J. Barnard
31 Stour Close
Strood
Rochester
Kent ME2 3JX

Moira Pedigree WRC
Mrs J. Roberts
2 Holywell Cottages
Burton Road
Ashby-de-la-Zouch
Leicestershire

Northern Pedigree WRC
Mr D. Smith
116 Lawsons Road
Thornton Clevelys
Blackpool
Lancashire FY5 4PX

South Cotswolds WRC
Mrs E. Hayes
1 Fourth Avenue
Dursley
Gloucestershire GL11 4NX

Stanborough WRC
Mrs P. Bawden
10 Homestead Court
Welwyn Garden City
Hertfordshire AL7 4LY

West Cornwall WRC
Mrs D. Rowe
8 Polstain Road
Threemilestone
Truro
Cornwall TR3 6DH

West Somerset WRC
Miss G. Harcombe
30 Pooles Close
Nether Stowey
Somerset TA5 1LZ

Whippet Coursing Club
    (Racing Section)
Mrs M. Scott
25 Riverhill
Worcester Park
Surrey KT4 7QB

Whippet Club of Scotland
Mr D. F. Lindsay
Manseburn
Kippen
Stirling
Scotland FK8 3EF

Appendix 3

Breed Clubs Outside the UK

USA

The American Whippet Club, Inc.
Secretary: Mrs Harriett N. Lee
14 Oak Circle
Charlottesville
Virginia 22901
USA

The Southern California
    Whippet Association
President: Mrs Ann Billups
421 Northhurst Avenue
Glandora
California 91740
USA

Canada

The Whippet Club of
    Eastern Canada
Secretary: Mrs M. Secord
1323 Kilbride Street
Kilbride
Ontario LOP 1GO
Canada

Stampede City Whippet Club
Secretary: Wynn T. Fellde
116 Queensland Drive SE
Calgary
Alberta T2J 3R7
Canada

France

Club Francais du Whippet
President: Dr Vet J. F. Moniot
130 Bis Avenue G. Pompidou
33500 Limbourne
France

Germany

Deutscher Windhundzucht-und
    Rennverband E.V.
Secretary: Mrs Ilse Hilz
Silvanerstrasse 16
6501 Jugenheim
West Germany

Sweden *

Svenska Whippetklubben
Secretary: Mrs Anna Tena
Backvall
Serstafors
73090 Kilback
Sweden

Belgium

Club Royal Belge du Levrier
President: Mrs L. Van Tongerloo-
    Janssens
Gijselstraat 80
2200 Borgerhout
Belgium

Holland

Nederlandse Whippet Club
Secretary: Mrs A. Smits-Geubels
Laan Van Heemstede 54
3297 A J Puttershoek
Holland

Italy

Club del Levriero
President: Mr G. Grandi
c/o Mrs A. Amaturo
Loc. Poggio n.3
61010 Fratte di Sassofeltrio (P.S.)
Italy

Bibliography

Bengtson, Bo, *The Whippet*, David & Charles, London (1985)

Daglish, E. Fitch, *The Whippet*, W. & G. Foyle, London (1964)

Douglas-Todd, C. H., *The Popular Whippet*, Popular Dogs Publising Co., London (1961)

Fitter, B. S., *The Show and Working Whippet*, printed by the East Anglian Daily Times (1940s)

Hutt, Frederick B., *Genetics For Dog Breeders*, W. H. Freeman and Company, San Francisco (1979)

Lloyd, Freeman S., *The Whippet or Race Dog*, The Bazaar Exchange & Mart Office, London (1894)

Pegram, Louis, *The Complete Whippet*, Howell Book House, New York (1976)

Renwick, W. Lewis, *The Whippet Handbook*, Nicholson & Watson, London (1957)

Russell, Joanna, *All About Gazehounds*, Pelham Books, London (1976) *Whippets: Sporting Bloodlines*, privately published (1983)

Walsh, E. G. and Lowe, Mary, *The English Whippet*, Boydell Press, Suffolk (1984)

Wilson, Pauline, *Whippets, Rearing and Racing*, Faber & Faber, London (1979)

Index